*A page turner full of history and humor...reveals the genesis of many of South Carolina's traditions, language and recipes, highlighting the far-reaching influence of the Scotch-Irish.*
*—Nathalie Dupree*
*Nationally acclaimed cookbook author and television host, founding chair of the Charleston Food and Wine Festival, a founder of Southern Foodways Alliance.*

❧

*I am glad that our ancestors were a part of this splendid community with its elevating and sustaining spiritual environment. I found a most impressive church that has served for close to two centuries as the center of spiritual life of a fine community of people. They have always shown many elements of true greatness. I am proud of the heritage that comes to us from such an ancestral line. I am proud of the present generation. I am glad that generally, the Mississippi and Texas clan have clung to the ideals and principles hewn out by the earlier members of the family.*
*—John C. Stennis*
*Fairview community Scotch-Irish descendant and U.S. senator, (D-MS 1947–89), now deceased*

❧

*Nothing was dearer to my father's heart than the proud Scotch-Irish heritage held together by kinship and close friendship across our Southern States! I, too, have witnessed the shared values and lifestyles of "the finest states in the Union."*
*—Margaret Stennis Womble*
*Daughter of Senator John Stennis*

❧

*I first "knew" Mrs. Caroline S. Coleman long before I met her. I knew her through the delightful pieces which she wrote about other times, other people and which were published in the Fountain Inn Tribune, Robert Quillen's paper.*
*I met, years later, the author of the pieces I so admired, a sprightly little lady, motherly, kind, perceptive...and exceedingly talented in putting down*

on paper reminiscences of another day. She agreed to do a twice-weekly column... They have been running in the Piedmont ever since and have attracted the greatest volume of congratulatory mail of any feature the Piedmont has run... This book is a collection of some of Mrs. Coleman's best pieces. They have delighted thousands of readers."
—William F. Gaines
*Editor,* Greenville Piedmont, *Greenville, South Carolina, 1962*

༄

*My thanks again for your article* [on our Scotch-Irish ancestors] *and your thoughtfulness.*
—Letter from W.C. Westmoreland to Caroline S. Coleman in 1969
General, U.S. Army, Chief of Staff

༄

*A valuable book for genealogists—historians—people searching for Scotch-Irish oral history.*
—Mark Paden
South Carolina Peden Clan historian

# Scotch-Irish Life
## in the
# SOUTH CAROLINA PIEDMONT

*Why They Wore Five Petticoats on Sunday*

MILLIE HUFF COLEMAN &
CAROLINE SMITH SHERMAN

THE
History
PRESS

Published by The History Press
Charleston, SC  29403
www.historypress.net

Original edition, *Five Petticoats on Sunday*
Copyright © 1962 by Caroline S. Coleman
Designed and Printed by Hiott Press, Greenville, SC
Drawings by Tommy Willis

*Cover*: Painting of *Historic Fairview Church*, James Taylor, artist. *Authors' family collections.*

First published 2014

ISBN 9781540210999

Library of Congress CIP data applied for.

*To the memory of our Scotch-Irish grandmother "Muzzy," Mary Caroline "Carrie" Sprouse Coleman, a strong Southern lady, widowed like her grandmother, mother and sister before her. She read the Bible for courage, raised and educated the children and managed the farm. Before marriage, she taught in a one-room schoolhouse. At age twenty-nine, she began a writing career that continued until her death at eighty-six.*

*She never drove a car but could handle a horse and buggy. She thought nothing of hopping on an airplane—a woman alone—to go to a convention to deliver a speech.*

*To the memory of her daughters: our aunt, Mary Agnes Coleman New, and our mothers, Marjorie "Margie" Casler Coleman Smith and Ina Jean Coleman Huff, also teachers, who stressed the importance of education and family. They encouraged us to pass the "history gene" to our children and grandchildren.*

*That is the purpose of this book.*
*—Marjorie Caroline Smith Sherman*
*and Mildred "Millie" Caroline Huff Coleman*
*2014*


*To the memory of my grandmother, Mary Stennis McKittrick, who was Scotch-Irish but more Scotch than Irish, a staunch Presbyterian, a Confederate widow never reconstructed.*

*And to my mother, Martha McKittrick Sprouse, willing to be reconstructed, but a little afraid of Grandma.*
*—Mary Caroline Sprouse Coleman*
*1962*

# Contents

## THE STORIES FROM *FIVE PETTICOATS ON SUNDAY*, PUBLISHED IN 1962
## 1860s-1890s

# 1900s (Naughts)

# "Bless Your Heart" and Many Thanks To:

Diane Bailey, owner of Bookquest in Fountain Inn, South Carolina: who urged us to do this book.

Henry Fulmer, director of the South Caroliniana Library, in Columbia and Caroline's Fountain Inn neighbor/friend in the Children of the Confederacy, Caroline S. Coleman Chapter: who gave us very good advice. His Scotch-Irish grandmother, Mrs. Emmie Stewart Fulmer: who was Caroline's "adopted, in-town grandmother."

Aunt Frances Coleman (wife of Uncle "Broad"), not blood kin but might as well be: whose reminiscences jogged our memories, inspiring us and her sons, our cousins: Sammy, Jackie, their wives and children.

Great-aunt Cinnie's prolific family, the Garretts, seventy-eight in all: who are so gracious when we come to visit and talk history. Gordon, the family genealogist/historian: who found pictures and more of the McKittricks and Sprouses.

Great-uncle Will Sprouse's Virginia family: who are now scattered to other states. We miss our cousin Carol and don't get to see you others often enough.

Brothers: "Buzzy" Smith: who is patient when we stay with him, bringing children, grandchildren and "Putty" cat. Johnny, Jimmy (and Paula), plus Joe and "Baby Sam" Huff: who were the first and youngest to go.

Sister Mary Agnes Huff: who is the most beautiful sister and a great public relations/writer too.

Our wonderful daughters, Mary Caroline, Liz and Carina: whose eyes glaze over sometimes when we are talking history or our work on the "book," but they still listen. Mary C., a writer like her great-grandmother, gave good suggestions.

New sons-in-law, Charles and Brent: whose eyes don't glaze over when we talk food and history. Yea-a-a, more Southerners in the family!

"Pip" Wood, almost a son-in-law, and almost a Southerner: whose eyes don't glaze over either.

Grandchildren John, Elizabeth, George and Aria, born in D.C and Texas: tenth matrilineal generation Scotch-Irish. Will they continue to come to Peden reunions in South Carolina, to play with their cousins, like we did?

Pittsburgh-born husband, Tom Coleman, no relation, until he married Millie: a fine, gentleman, but whose only interest in Scotch-Irish is golf.

Our English, German and Italian in-laws: who help us see the uniqueness of being Scotch-Irish, especially Peg, teaching Millie to sauté turnip greens in olive oil and garlic.

Katie Morgan: who donated the Civil War costumes we wear when we tell Scotch-Irish/Southern stories to groups.

Bert Hobby: who walked and talked this book.

Laura Nalesnik: the genius of MouseWhiskers Studio.

Susan Bohannan: who corrected our form and format from Virginia, retyping it all.

Mark Paden, the Peden clan historian, and Jackie Peden, the Peden clan secretary: who provided a wealth of Scotch-Irish and Peden information. Same kinship, but two different Paden spellings.

Local Pedens and Fairview Church members: who keep Scotch-Irish traditions/history and put on the reunion for more than 250 kinfolk every year. We can't say enough "thank-yous" to these good people.

Fountain Inn, "The Best Little Town in South Carolina" and Carrollton, the best in Georgia, where we grew up and visited each other.

Fairview friends and family members: whose names and photographs could not be included for time and space constraints.

# About This Book

This 2014 book reveals why they wore five—not just three—petticoats on Sunday, how toothbrushes grew on trees and what they did when they were "goin' over town" for Saturday shopping and fun. This was Scotch-Irish Southern life with its frequently strict, Presbyterian customs in the historic Fairview, South Carolina community. This land borders the current Greenville/Simpsonville/Fountain Inn superhighway. These roads were the stagecoach trails of yesteryear.

These oral histories highlight the 1890s to 1900s, also called the Victorian era or the Nineties and "Naughts" by these Scotch-Irish descendants. This was the generation after the Civil War. Countless historical works focus on men in war or politics, but this book spotlights daily living, especially from the women's and children's point of view.

Fairview was merely one community of Scotch-Irish pioneers—middle-class folk, with smaller farms and few slaves. However, in our experience and historical research, these Upcountry South Carolinians mirror the day-to-day life of other Scotch-Irish and Protestant immigrants who settled in rural farming communities between the coast and mountains.

Their Scotch-Irish idioms, as well as their social and religious customs, differed from those of Lowcountry plantation owners and urban Charleston contemporaries, especially those members of the hated Church of England.

These Presbyterian Piedmont settlers also contrasted with Appalachian Mountain clans and rambunctious Scottish Highlanders.

This book recalls the fun and lore of midland South Carolina, much like *The Foxfire Book* did for the northeast Georgia mountains. However, unlike reclusive mountain folk who stayed in the hills and hollows, these Scotch-Irish residents spread out. They generated Protestant descendants who form the bedrock of the eight-state Southern Piedmont today. Their Scotch-Irish traditions are what make the South so "Southern."

## ANCESTORS AND FAIRVIEW'S FOUNDING FAMILIES

In the 1600s, Peden the Prophet, from Ayrshire, Scotland, inspired Presbyterian Scottish and Scotch-Irish Covenanters to follow their Scottish faith, despite hardship and persecution. Peden's fiery sermons urged them to reject England's foreign power and its Church of England, as well as Ireland's Catholic "papists." During the 1770s, when Scotch-Irish land leases expired in Northern Ireland, one Covenanter Presbyterian took charge. Reverend Martin filled five shiploads with Scotch-Irish Presbyterian families. Babies to old folks left Ballymena Parish, County Antrim, Northern Ireland. They aimed for South Carolina, seeking more religious freedom and less government restriction in the new American colonies.

Since Ellis Island didn't open for immigration until 1890, Reverend Martin's immigrants entered Charleston Harbor at Sullivan's Island. They received land grants and eventually built homes in the Piedmont. This is also called the Upcountry in South Carolina. They cleared these slightly rolling midlands between the coast and the mountains, a reminder of the "auld" landscapes of Scotland and Ireland. They established the Fairview Presbyterian Church and the Fairview community.

The first Fairview church included members by the names of Peden, Alexander, Gaston, Morton and Nesbit. A second wave followed with Andersons, Hopkins, Woodsides, McKittricks, Stewarts and Martins. They were joined by the Stenhouse and Stennis families, who were "Border Scots." They originated from Kirk Yetholm, in Scotland, on the tempestuous lands near the English border. These Fairview founders, along with their Baptist and Methodist neighbors, instilled their conservative, biblical traditions and Protestant preachin', thus prompting the term the "Bible Belt" for the South.

Liam Neeson, present-day movie star of films such as *Schindler's List*, is a modern Ballymena boy. He hails from the Pedens' old community in County Antrim, Northern Ireland. According to BBC interviews, though Irish Catholic, he, too, was influenced by the fiery Scotch-Irish Presbyterian preachin' before he came to America.

Soon, other Scotch-Irish families arrived, joining their kin and former neighbors. As Fairview's families grew, some moved on, eventually populating the whole Southern Piedmont. As they settled in Georgia, Alabama, Mississippi and Texas, they honored their old Ballymena Fairview church. The pioneers christened several new churches "Fairview Presbyterian" as their wagons rolled westward across the Piedmont. An Internet search will show you where all these Fairview churches are today.

This book illustrates the impact of Scotch-Irish immigration and kinship. The Fairview community's Peden Clan spawned countless preaching and teaching descendants, as well as unsung heroines and forgotten heroes. At huge clan gatherings, attendees stand to be counted and acknowledged from John and Peggy McDill Peden's seven sons and three daughters: the "House of Mary," "House of James," etc. You may recognize two twenty-first-century Peden descendants: U.S. Senator John C. Stennis (Mississippi), of the House of Alexander, and U.S. Army Major General William C. Westmoreland (South Carolina), of the House of Thomas. The authors also descend from the House of Alexander.

Our maternal grandmother, "Muzzy," was Mary Caroline "Carrie" Sprouse Coleman (House of Alexander). She grew up in the Fairview community in the 1880s and was immersed in the family stories. This led to extensive historical research and countless publications, including 1950s *Greenville Piedmont* newspaper columns titled "Away Back When." She recounted Scotch-Irish history in her 1962 book, *Five Petticoats on Sunday*.

After she died in 1969, her book went out of print. Language changed, along with hats and Sunday dress codes. However, she summoned us posthumously in the books she signed, instructing us: "To Grand-daughter Mildred who loves the old stories," and "To Caroline, my oldest granddaughter...someday you will pass these reminiscences on to another generation."

It's high time. It has been over one hundred years since these events happened in the Fairview community—our, and possibly your, Scotch-Irish ancestors' home. We decided to republish her stories exactly as she wrote them, to capture the dialect and flavor of the 1800s. However since modern readers may be baffled by her terms, we tried to define as many as we could, beginning with "Scotch-Irish."

# Recognizing the Scotch-Irish

The South Carolina Scotch-Irish have always called themselves Scotch-Irish, not *Scots*-Irish. This term, Scotch-Irish, has been used for three hundred years. In the United States, it refers to the Scots who immigrated to Great Britain's Ulster Province in Northern Ireland. This land is on the same island but is a different political entity from today's Republic of Ireland. These Scots stayed for several generations before coming to American colonies in migratory waves during the 1770s and 1800s. This was decades before Ireland's Great (potato) Famine.

Scotch-Irish is only one of multiple descriptive terms. In Northern Ireland, they say Ulster Scots. In the United States, ethnic heritage groups and scholars hotly debate their favorite designations: i.e., Scottish-Irish, Scots-Irish and Scotch-Irish American, to name a few.

Edinburgh, Scotland historian (and our cousin) Bruce Stenhouse reprimanded us for saying "Scotch-Irish." He declared, "Scotch is whisky! Scots are the people of Scotland."

Despite his lecture, in this book, we will stick to Scotch-Irish. Why? Because that's what most Scotch-Irish settlers, including our maternal great-great-grandmother, Grandma McKittrick, and her Fairview neighbors called themselves. Their descendants still identify themselves this way, despite marrying into other ethnic groups.

As a college graduate and educator, Mrs. Coleman was determined to use only the most proper and kindly terms of the era. Please understand that any archaic, racial and/or gendered phrases in "The Stories" section were politically and grammatically correct in her day. It was a different world in her Scotch-Irish "Nineties and Naughts." No disrespect was or is, intended.

Social upheavals have changed the South, influencing everyone's descendants. Today, there is curiosity and renewed discourse about the subtle differences in the peoples who settled the South. There is revivalist pride in ethnic heritage, Southern food, genealogy and cultural roots. We expect that you will discover unacknowledged Scotch-Irish habits, language and religious beliefs in "The Stories" section of this book.

"The Glossary" chapter defines amusing and outdated 1800s vernacular. "The Scotch-Irish Terms and Phrases" section will help translate, and enrich, the meaning of being Scotch-Irish and "Southern." For example, if a friend points "over yonder," we hope you will acknowledge, "Ah-hah. She has a Scotch-Irish heritage."

Or when colleagues say, "I reckon," they are really speaking proper Scottish, not English, phrases. If your co-worker answers, "I might could go with you," or complains, "He's so nebby!" they are speaking "auld" Scottish for "maybe or possibly" and "He's very nosy, curious and interfering."

We put in a few very old dishes, once called "receipts," for you to try in the "Scotch-Irish Receipts (Recipes)" section. There are images of old homeplaces and Scotch-Irish Fairview families. We hope you'll laugh *with* us—not *at* their dour expressions. Unlike today, old-time photographers instructed them *not* to smile.

# HUNGRY FOR MORE?

In the 1950s, our elders—Muzzy and her sister, Cinnie—recited Fairview ancestry on the big front porch, while the lightning bugs blinked. They wanted their namesake granddaughters Marjorie Caroline, Mildred Caroline, Mary Agnes and Mary Anderson to remember every kinship story and cousin's name, especially those attending the Fairview Church, Peden Clan and Sprouse reunions.

If your elders are gone or your family has scattered, leaving no genealogical records, check our "Resources" section. We've listed lesser-known books and websites about the Scotch-Irish. There are over twenty thousand Fairview descendants' names; their immigration, land grants and military details; plus town and church histories. Visit the Fountain Inn History Center on Depot Street for centuries of Scotch-Irish exhibits—including Mrs. Caroline S. "Muzzy" Coleman's velvet hat and typewriter.

You are welcome to meet Scotch-Irish cousins from all over the United States at the annual Peden Clan Reunion. It's the third Sunday in July at the historic Fairview Presbyterian Church in Fountain Inn. Just bring a dish or a story to share.

# Message from Mrs. Caroline S. Coleman, 1962 Edition Author

This book is a collection of published columns. Many requests from readers of the column, which appears in the *Greenville Piedmont*, "wanting to buy a book of your columns," led to this volume.

The book grew out of reminiscences related by my grandmother on long winter evenings as we sat around the fireside, the soft light of a lightwood-knot fire shining on our eager youthful faces.

"Grandma, please tell us about the war and about when you were a little girl" would start Grandma back along the pathway of history. She was never to know that every word would be treasured by one small listener and would someday inspire that history-loving granddaughter to pass on her own memories, centering around life with Grandma.

Many volumes have been written featuring the romance and glamor of plantation life in the Southern Lowcountry. Much has been written in recent years about the mountain regions of the South, including the mountain folks, their philosophy and way of life. Comparatively little has been written about life in the Piedmont, the fertile region between the foothills and the level lands below the fall line. The Piedmont was settled by hardy Scotch-Irish pioneers who came down the mountain passes from Pennsylvania and Virginia, following the Catawba Path and the Great Wagon Road, to wrest homes from the Upcountry forests.

Here they braved the Indian tomahawk to clear patches in the wilderness, raise log cabin homes and kindle their altar fires in one-room, log meetinghouses. By dint of rigid economy and hard work, the Scotch-Irish prospered. Eventually, substantial homes replaced the log cabins, and stately country churches replaced the log cabin meetinghouses.

The settlement's social—as well as spiritual—life centered around the country church. For six days, the Scotch-Irish labored along with their servants, but the Sabbath was for the worship of the Lord in their churches. Master and servant and their households observed the Sabbath in almost biblical manner.

Life was good in the rural Piedmont in the Nineties and Naughts. The South was still staggering from the effects of the Sixties, but young people who had never known anything save strict economy did not miss luxuries they had never known. And despite the almost Puritan code that governed our lives, we had good times and fun.

Mrs. Caroline "Carrie" Coleman signing her first book, *Five Petticoats on Sunday*. *Authors' family collection.*

"Mother," my children kept saying to me, "unless you write down these stories of life when you were young, our children will never know how people lived in the strange world that you remember." Thus, we have tried to picture country life in the Piedmont in the Nineties and Naughts.

The late Robert Quillen, internationally known writer, first used my little column in the *Fountain Inn Tribune*, the weekly newspaper that he published as a hobby. Finally, Judson W. Chapman of the *Greenville Piedmont* began to use my stories of "Away Back When," and in time, William F. Gaines, present editor of the *Piedmont*, asked me to submit the stories in column form.

From the beginning of my venture as a columnist, the response has been most generous and surprising.

It is customary to thank all who have helped a writer in preparing a book. I wish I had space to thank all of you and mention your names. A big drawer in my desk is filled with letters from readers who have written to say they like the column. You have encouraged me in far greater measure than you know. Thank you, indeed, each and all of you.

I want to thank especially editor William Gaines, who requested the column and who has gone far beyond the line of duty in encouraging me. Without his inspiration, there would have been no column. Thank you, especially, to Mrs. William P. Barton, the "Polly Piedmont," kind friend and editor, who has given me many a boost by her interest and enthusiasm. Thank you to Wayne Freeman, one of the first to say, "I like very much your stories of the old times." Thank you to all the editors of woman's department and other editors and the staff of the *Piedmont* who have never let me down.

Thank you, too, to the *Greenville News*, especially to B.H. Peace Jr. and Jim Walker. Had it not been for Jim Walker's insistence, I should not have ventured to compile the columns in book form.

Thank you to my friends in Fountain Inn for their encouragement, especially Mark Nelson, who has suffered my stories in varied forms to appear in the *Tribune* all these years and has never grown impatient.

And in memoriam, I want to express my thanks to the late Judson Chapman, who gave me my start, and the late Robert Quillen—except for him, my memories might never have appeared in print.

The Stories from *Five Petticoats on Sunday*, Published in 1962

1860s-1890s

*Chapter 1*

# Five Petticoats on Sunday

Three plain petticoats could make do on weekdays when no strangers were around to suspect how many limbs a lady had above her ankles, but we wore five petticoats on Sunday. Our Sunday petticoats were made of white domestic, with ruffles of lace and embroidery. Times were hard in the not-so-gay Nineties. The South was still staggering from the blows of the Sixties; cotton was selling for five cents the pound. We had no money for silk stockings or other foolishness, but we had to have money for lace and embroidery for trimming our Sunday petticoats. Come the Sabbath morning and time to dress for going to the meetinghouse, we would don our quota of stiffly starched petticoats, no matter how warm the weather.

"I'll no have a huzzy in my family," Grandma said sternly when we pleaded to leave off just one of the petticoats on a sultry summer day. And in Grandma's code, only a huzzy would rustle down the aisle of the meetinghouse on Sunday with fewer than five petticoats covering her limbs.

We were never able to find in the big Bible any reference to the matter of wearing petticoats on Sunday, but Grandma was Scotch-Irish and more Scotch than Irish, and in life with Grandma, there was no compromising. What we wore and what we did on the Sabbath Day was regulated by a code as strict as the Decalogue.

There was the matter of reading. We read only the Bible and "Sunday books" on the Sabbath Day.

"Please, Grandma, may I read the book on the top shelf?" A little girl of eleven years, with freckled face and big brown eyes, looked pleadingly at

Grandma. I had read over and over the old brown leather-covered books in Great-Grandfather's library—*Scottish Chiefs*, *Lady of the Manor*, *Ivanhoe*, *Pilgrim's Progress* and others beyond my years. More keen than a hunger for bread, I hungered for something to read. Only one book in the old mahogany book case had been denied me, a book with a queer name: *Don Quixote*.

"Please, please, Grandma, let me read *Don Quixit*," I begged. Raising her steel-rimmed spectacles to her forehead, Grandma peered at the top shelf, then reluctantly took down the old volume and placed it in my eager hands.

"My child, you may read the book if you will give me your promise that you will read it only on Wednesdays and Thursdays," she said.

"But why, Grandma?" My eyes opened wide in wonder.

"It is a worldly book, my child, and I fear it may be sinful to read it. The book was given to my father. Father, himself, would read it only on Wednesdays and Thursdays—the days farthest from the Sabbath.

Thus, at the age of eleven years, I read *Don Quixote*—halfway between Sundays.

"Put away the weekly newspaper, the *Youth's Companion* and the farm paper," Grandma would say on Saturday afternoon. All week long, we had been getting ready for Sunday. Little girls' frocks and petticoats were crisply starched and ironed, and stiff-bosomed shirts worn by the menfolk on Sunday were made immaculate by much labor. Shoes must be polished and buttons sewed on. If a little girl forgot to sew a missing button on her Sunday shoes, she had to go to church with that button missing, a painful experience that she remembered next time.

Nearly all cooking was done on Saturday. We ate hot breakfast on Sunday but cold dinner and supper, simple fare at that. The sound of the coffee grinder in the afternoon told us that it was Saturday, as Mother never forgot to grind a supply of coffee to last over Sunday, like manna that fell in the wilderness. The sound of the churn dasher thumping was missing on Sunday, and the sound of the axe was missing from the woodpile. Nobody cut wood on Sundays.

On Sunday morning, we were up early, for it was a long drive to our church. Only necessary chores were attended to—feeding the stock, milking the cows. When the shining buggy or surrey had been brought to the door, we were ready in our Sunday frocks and petticoats for the drive along a dusty or muddy road, our clothing protected by winter or summer lap robes. There would be the long sermon, and we had to sit without fidgeting. We must not go to sleep for fear of the peach tree switch that would await us when we returned home.

How many petticoats did she wear in 1904? Mary Caroline "Carrie" Sprouse, book author, in lace-trimmed, white college graduation dress. *Authors' family collection.*

*From left to right*: Lucinda "Cinnie" Hopkins; widowed mother, Martha Jane "Mattie" McKittrick Sprouse, age thirty-two; William "Will" Warren; and Caroline "Carrie," age twelve in 1895. *Authors' family collection.*

Sunday afternoons were long. We were required to learn Scripture verses, the Catechism and hymns. After this, we might walk about the yard quietly without noise or romping. We were permitted to sit in the swing but not to do any swinging. Should we begin to joggle the swing, we were certain to hear reproof: "My child, this is the Lord's Day."

The few toys we had were put away on Saturday night. It was sinful to even pick up a doll or a ball. There were two things Grandma welcomed about as much as she would have welcomed a rattlesnake in her home: the Sunday newspaper and the sight of children playing games on Sunday.

A relative living a long distance from the church might stop by our house on the way from church and share our cold dinner. Then, after feeding his horse, he would drive on. Only in the case of grave illness did any of the kinfolks come for a visit on Sunday. When we heard the rumble of wagon wheels on Sunday, we hurried to look out at the road to find who of our neighbors had died on Sunday. Only when there was a death in his family did a farmer ever drive to town on a Sunday—to bring back a casket in his wagon.

How rapidly the times have changed. When we recently heard a minister announce that his sermon would be on "Sabbath Observance," we sat up to listen. But when he began with "I read in this morning's newspaper…", we groaned inwardly. The man knew nothing about Sabbath-keeping.

The two little girls who wore the five petticoats on Sunday and their younger brother—Caroline, Lucinda and William, shortened to Carrie, Cinnie and Will—grew up in the amazing era described in these columns. They reached their teens before they learned that there were families in the world who did not observe the Sabbath in the Scotch-Irish way and who thought nothing of serving syllabub spiked with spirits instead of plain boiled custard for Christmas Dinner.

## Chapter 2

# "Prophet's Room" — Always Ready

The "Prophet's Room" was included in all building plans for homes in this section of the Piedmont in the early nineteenth century. After the horseback preachers had become only a memory, the room that had been dedicated to their use was known as the "piazza room." The word "porch" had a northern sound. Southerners said "piazza."

The Scotch-Irish who raised log cabin homes in the Piedmont replaced these later with homes in keeping with the growing prosperity. Sherman's army bypassed lower Greenville County, and consequently, the sturdy old homes were still little changed at the turn of the century.

Still standing in the lower part of the county is possibly the oldest of these homes. Here my grandmother was born and lived out most of her life. Built by her father, John Stennis, in 1808, according to the date imprinted on the mortar of the chimney, the house followed the typical building plan of that day. It was a two-story building of logs, weatherboarded over with stout siding. The logs were cut from virgin forests on the place; the building was done by means of slave labor, as was the case with other homes of the period.

Chimneys at each end of the house were important, as the chimney at the living room end of the home faced the road. Windows at each side of the chimney gave a view of the road and passersby interested in the family.

There was a piazza at both the front and rear of the house. The front piazza faced the garden, with its boxwoods and blooming shrubbery, while the back piazza looked out on the out-kitchen nearby and the neat cabins

The "Prophet's Room" is on the left in the 1808 John/Rebecca Peden Stennis home. Sons Alexander and Adam moved to Mississippi in the Peden cousins' wagon train in the 1830s. *Authors' family collection.*

in the distance for the servants. One end of each piazza was enclosed to form a bedroom. The bedroom at the end of the front piazza was the "prophet's room."

In this small room, there was a fireplace, where wood and kindling were always laid in winter. The big four-poster was piled high with a feather bed, over which were soft quilts, along with fat pillows and a bolster. There was a high chest of drawers and a washstand with bowl and pitcher, all provided for the comfort of the prophet.

Before the dawn of the nineteenth century, when there were few settlements in this section of the South, ministers rode horseback from as far away as New York, visiting hamlets where a group might assemble to hear the gospel and a little church would later be constructed. Even in the early 1800s, preachers with Bibles in saddlebags were still making the rounds in rural areas of America. Any horseback preacher would feel free to enter the prophet's room of a Southern home and find rest and sleep in a big feather bed. When possible, the preacher entered without disturbing the family members, and the next morning, when the bearded prophet appeared at their breakfast table, they were surprised to find that they had entertained an angel unaware.

Grandma often told the story of the hardships the horseback preachers had to endure and how when such a rider came in sight of a home with a prophet's chamber, it was a welcome sight, possibly even a lifesaver on a cold, rainy night. Some of the inns in sections reached by the stage road were not deemed fitting places for lodging a minister of the gospel. Then, much of the route traversed by the horseback preacher was far from the stage road. Only the Southern homes with their well-known prophet's chambers made it possible for the rugged preachers to "open up" the wilderness with the gospel. Fording the streams, miring up to their horses' knees in mud and facing driving rains, the prophets riding the trails were unsung heroes of their generation.

## Chapter 3

# Threshing Time in the Nineties

June was wheat-threshing month in the Nineties and Naughts. Could be that one of the girls wanting a June wedding had to consider the threshers and when they would come. The menfolk grumbled at the very mention of a June wedding. "Can't tell what day the threshers will come, and wheat has got to be threshed when the threshers can come—wedding or no wedding."

When wheat was ripe, it was not a matter of driving the power combine over the field and loading the threshed wheat. A big, cumbersome threshing machine pulled by a steam engine went the rounds of the neighborhood when the wheat was ready for threshing. The owner of the machinery, called the "boss," had a list of the farms, and he would send word ahead when he would reach the first farm on his list and then move on to the next until all had been reached.

When word came to our place that the thresher was on the way, it was an exciting time. A mighty stirring began. We children were dispatched to pick blackberries or to pick up apples from under the trees to go into pies—"and hurry," we were admonished. We wanted to hurry to get back to see what was going on. The kitchen was a beehive of activity as Mother and the colored women aided by Grandma prepared a huge dinner. Chickens were hastily made ready for chicken pies; big baskets of beans were strung and put on to cook with plenty of potatoes. A thick, tender ham was cut and big slices put in frying pans.

In the meantime, we had heard the rumbling of the approaching engine that came creaking down the road, with the threshing machine following

The Nash Mill in Fairview Community looked like this Jones Mill, which remains outside Fountain Inn today. After threshing, grain was sent to a mill like this to be ground into flour. *Artist Art Frahm.*

along. From our perch on the barnyard fence, we would watch the proceedings as the wagons came along loaded with equipment, the thresher hands riding on top.

With much puffing and blowing off steam and tooting of the whistle, the big engine would be placed at the right spot. The boss would shout at the men to get to their places, and Big Ellick, the engineer in garb like a pirate, with a red bandana around his neck, would handle his engine, readying it for the task. Wagons loaded with bundles of wheat were driving in from the fields where the wheat had been shocked. All the farmhands were laboring to get the bundles ready for the business of threshing.

With final hissing of steam and shouting from the boss, the roar of the thresher would begin. One man ran the thresher, other men fed the bundles into the machine's big maw, others on the ground threw the bundles to the feeders and still others held bags to catch the steady stream of golden grain pouring from the machine. Who would have thought the day would come when a machine would whir around in the field and achieve the whole thing in one process?

When the dinner bell rang, the men gathered around the well in the yard to wash their faces and hands and then all trooped gladly into the house. One long table in the dining room and another in the kitchen would be groaning with chicken pies, apple and blackberry pies, country ham, vegetables, hot biscuits and cornbread, pounds of golden butter, pitchers of buttermilk and pots of coffee. A continual laughing and joking went on as the men ate, and from the kitchen came the sound of good-natured fun, which was all part of the thresher's daily rounds.

If there were not too many breakdowns, and if time were not lost by having to send to town for parts to replace broken gadgets, the job would be done before night, and word would be sent to the next neighbor to prepare supper for the thresher hands. With much noise and activity, the engine and its accompanying load would slowly pull out of the yard, and we children were sad to see them go. Threshing time was almost like Christmas with its excitement.

*Chapter 4*

# The Old Smokehouse

The passing of the old-time smokehouse is noticeable as you drive over the rural section of the South. A familiar sight in the backyard of every rural home away back when was the stout structure with a heavy door and tiny window, without which no farm home was complete.

The pioneers built smokehouses out of logs, and some of the old log smokehouses lasted for generations. When these had deteriorated, farmers built strong frame smokehouses with low eaves, after the original pattern. The smokehouse invariably had a dirt floor, hard packed and dark with age and smoke stains. No other floor would serve, for the fires of hickory logs and chips were laid on the dirt floor.

Suspended above the fire were the big hams, shoulders and sides of the huge hogs grown on the farm in that day. A slow smoke from the smoldering hickory enveloped the meat and darkened the entire room. The fire was kept burning day and night for the required period of "curing" the meat. Then the fire was allowed to go out, but the aroma of hickory smoke and seasoned meat never left the smokehouse. When we opened the door of Grandma's smokehouse, even in midsummer, there was the tangy fragrance of smoked hams.

The smokehouse odor recalled stories of the Sixties when salt was almost impossible to obtain. "We dug up the dirt right here," Grandma told us, "and tried to separate the dirt from the salt that had dripped from the meat in all the years before." It sounded unappetizing to hear of getting salt from dirt, but when families in the Sixties butchered the few pigs they had grown, they were desperately in need of salt for preserving the precious meat supply. Even a little bit of salt was helpful. No housewife of that day ever forgot digging up the smokehouse floor for salt.

After being cured, the meat in the smokehouse was stored in barrels or hung suspended in big bags from the joists overhead. There were muslin bags stuffed with sausage hanging from the rafters. Sometimes the men would kill a beef, and neighbors divided the quarters. A quarter would be suspended from the joists of the smokehouse, where it would gradually dry out and cure. When meat was needed for meals, Grandma would take a sharp knife and go to the smokehouse, where she sliced a liberal supply of ham from a pig or steak from the quarter of beef, or she would bring in a bag of sausage. One gets nostalgic in recalling the sight of a pan filled with wide slices of pink ham fresh from the smokehouse or the dried sausage sizzling in the frying pan.

Finally, the custom of home smoking of meat was outmoded. Farmers salt-cured their meat without smoke or, in some cases, used preparations of smoke-flavored salt, which were good and meant that less labor was required for finishing the job. The aroma of hickory smoke still hung over the dark interior of the smokehouse, even when the meat was cured by other methods.

Hanging from the rafters, too, would be pokes of herbs—sage, marjoram, tansy and the like—strings of peppers and pokes of seeds for planting. The stout walls of the smokehouse prevented things from freezing in the coldest weather, so that was a good place to store the canned fruit and many other commodities.

In a corner near the door stood the molasses barrel with the supply of black molasses. On Saturday afternoon, the farmhands brought their jugs for molasses. The barrel would go back to town in the wagon when a refill was needed. The fragrance of black molasses also hung over the room, mingling with that of smoked meat.

The modern "smokehouse" is a huge white freezer in nearly every home. The housewife opens the freezer and takes out a supply of food that Grandma never dreamed would be available except in its regular season. And who could want to go back to the good old days of the smokehouse with such a marvelous invention as the deep freezer at hand?

*Chapter 5*

# The Day of the Long Johns

## Shedding the Heavies

**W**arm days in February are false harbingers of spring. There is still plenty of cold weather yet, according to an infallible prophet. Didn't the groundhog see his shadow on Candlemas Day? Then, as our grandparents would have assured us, "six more weeks of winter yet to come."

Six weeks from the day dedicated to the groundhog would only land us in the middle of March, and as everyone knows, March is no time to be thinking about shedding the "heavies."

"What do you mean 'shedding the heavies'?" a youngster asked. And we are reminded in emphatic terms that nobody wears any heavy underwear any more, or outerwear either, except for fur coats, or cashmere or tweed. The girls step out in sleeveless frocks that sing of spring, don coats to cover up their frocks and, arriving at a party or dinner, shed the coats. Nobody can tell it is winter by looking at the frocks, shoes and hose.

Shoes, even in winter, are merely a few straps of fancy leather, and gossamer hose don't keep frostbite away. Strange that we never hear of chilblains these days, but back in the Nineties when girls wore comparatively stout shoes, buttoned up with shiny buttons, and their hosiery was black cotton-ribbed numbers, we heard of many cases of frostbitten heels.

Strange to say, we didn't know then that it was possible to go out in midwinter with heels and toes sticking out and practically nothing in the way of stockings. The very suggestion of such a thing would have brought on symptoms of pneumonia, or at least our mothers would have thought so.

"You'll catch your death," we were told if we started out on a buggy ride to a party, to church or elsewhere without the full quota of red flannels, woolen suits and coats, with head swathed in a fascinator for evening wear or heavily veiled hats for daytime.

Girls wore red flannel petticoats under their ruffled taffetas, and boys wore flannel long johns, even when spring was in the air. Warm days made flannels almost unbearable, and the babies fretted and whined in discomfort, with red flannel next to their tender skin.

"False spring," our mothers would say, when such days as we have had in February this year came around. Even in April there was no trusting the weather. Fickle spring would keep flirting around—now you would see her, now you didn't—so we had to be content to wear the heavies until the first of May.

Came May Day, and it was spring. Rain or shine, wet weather or not, we got into lace and embroidered nainsook and hung the red flannels on the line. Off came the long johns, and the boys were happy to have them on the line instead of scratching the skin. Off came heavy ribbed hosiery, and stepping out in spring wearables was something.

May first could be cold and rainy. A fire might be needed in the living room, or we would be found huddling around the kitchen stove, but no matter. By the calendar, spring had come to stay, and there was no more danger of catching our deaths.

Until May 1, Grandma still kept the red flannel cloth that she had soaked in tallow and turpentine for such emergencies as quinsy or pleurisy, or even a deep-seated cold. Nothing would take the place of the red flannel to place on throat or chest when there was illness of this nature. And the old tallow-coated square would not be discarded until real hot weather came. Then it would be burned, and early next fall, another would be made ready for home use.

Let the poets sing of the buds and flowers, the daffodils and zephyrs of spring, but unless they have experienced the bliss of shedding the heavies, they know nothing about the marvels of spring.

## Chapter 6

# The Old-Time "Wash Place"

The old-time "wash place," once so much a part of every rural home, has gone the way of the side saddle and spinning wheel. Ask a modern youngster about the wash place, and you will be queried in turn, "What is that?"

There was a little stream or even a spring near every home, and the wash place was on a site nearby. A wooden trough built long and narrow served to convey water from the spring or from a clear pool in the stream to a big tub placed beneath the end of the trough. A stout wooden bench for holding the row of tubs, another bench for a "battling bench" and the two large iron pots or kettles for boiling the clothes made up the equipment used in the old-fashioned laundry, the outdoor wash place. Sometimes the wash place was in a sheltered or shady spot in the backyard, but in Grandma's day, there was always a spring or a branch for the purpose.

Early in the morning on wash day, the colored washerwoman to whom we belonged started a fire under the iron pots. Every family was possessed by a washerwoman, whose moods influenced family life. If our "Aunt Betsy" was cheerful and in a mood for washing, the week would be started off right.

The fire crackling and the smoke rising from the direction of every wash place in the neighborhood was a good sign on Monday morning. Aunt Betsy would shoulder the big pack of clothes tied up in a sheet and hasten to her task. Swishing and rubbing the clothes through a tub of steaming suds, she would sing the spirituals and keep time with the rub a dub, dub on the rub board. Into the black pot of more suds, the clothes would be tossed; and she would keep up a frequent stirring with the battling stick.

Did you ever see a "battling stick"? It was a long-handled wooden paddle, something like a baseball bat, and when the clothes had boiled long enough, Aunt Betsy would lift the clothes, a few pieces at a time, out of the boiling water and deposit the garments on the battling bench. Then she proceeded to flail them with the battling stick to "get the dirt out." It worked; when the soiled overalls and towels were well treated with the battling stick, they were clean and clear, but it was hard on materials and death to buttons on shirts.

The wash place was always kept swept clean of trash, and the sparkling water running through the trough made it a pleasant place for play. Washing was all done in one day, just once a week. In summer, the fire burned nearly all the day with such mounds of things like white frocks and shirts and petticoats to fill the tubs. Everybody wore cotton, and everything was washable.

The good old washerwomen began to disappear, and the younger ones were seldom satisfactory. No matter how much they needed the money, they were not faithful and dependable as were those in other days. Possibly this was the deciding factor in the disappearance of the wash place. Salesmen found that Southern women were open to persuasion, and they moved in with sales talk and demonstrations of the electric washing machine. Soon, there was in every home a gleaming machine to replace the Aunt Betsys, and kilowatt power took over the job formerly accomplished by elbow grease.

## Chapter 7

# The Surrey with the Fringe

The surrey with a fringe top and showy glass lamps on either side up near the top was a stylish conveyance in the Nineties.

The shiny surrey was invariably a black job, top and all, but the fringe, which gracefully festooned the top and hung down for several inches to wave gently with the motion of the vehicle, was a beige shade to match the covering of the seats. The lamps, something on the order of pin-up lamps, were black, with bright metal fittings and with clear glass frontage that reflected the acetylene torches within.

It was a great day when the worn, double-seated buggy had been traded in for the new surrey, and the magnificent vehicle in all its newness was placed in the carriage house to be carefully guarded against dust or inclement weather. The harness, of course, had to be new and with gleaming metal trimmings, and before old Dobbin was hitched to the surrey, he had been groomed with care as befitting the new outfit.

The lap robe was carefully folded on the back seat of the surrey when we were ready for the drive. The summer lap robe was of crash or linen, dust colored with a colored border and fringe. In winter, we had a heavy, wooly robe that was equivalent to two blankets. This was nearly always black or maroon, with plenty of decorative touches, such as a big bear in an outstanding color appliqued on the center of the robe and matching colors used in the border.

The surrey was open to the air, but under the back seat was a compartment designed to hold the "storm curtains." The stiff, black curtains of oilcloth

An 1880s surrey, equivalent in luxury to a Cadillac car today. *Artist Tommy Willis.*

had "windows" of isinglass, and when we had been shut in, with the storm windows buttoned around the top of the surrey, the isinglass windows let in a vague light. Shiny little buttons around the top and sides of the vehicle and corresponding buttonholes in the storm curtains were designed to convert the open-air conveyance into a kind of limousine.

The trouble with such an arrangement was the likelihood of a hard shower catching us before we could get the curtains up. Driving smoothly along, we would watch the approaching clouds, hoping that we could get ahead of the rain and reach home in time. But suddenly, drops would begin to pelt down, and we hastily vacated the back seat, withdrew the folded storm curtains and shook them out. With rain coming down faster, the buttons and buttonholes would grow contrary and give us all kinds of trouble. Finally, by the time the buttonholes had been matched to the buttons, we were all soaked from the shower. We retreated into the dark recess of the surrey and sat shivering behind the smelly oilcloth curtains, while in most cases, the shower had ended by the time we had the curtains up.

In very cold weather, we often put up the curtains before starting on the drive, and we found it hard to decide whether we preferred being exposed to biting winds in the open surrey or sitting in gloomy darkness surrounded by oilcloth and isinglass.

## Chapter 8

# The Coffee Grinder

**W**e notice more people taking "coffee breaks" than usual, and we love the thought of a coffee break. It sounds so warm and comforting and spirit uplifting—the coffee break in the morning when the first weary feeling begins to creep up on one, and again in the afternoon, when you just can't make it until night without a cup of coffee for a pickup.

America has been a nation of coffee drinkers from early days. Only in the South in the Sixties were people forced to forego their coffee. Ersatz coffee—a dark liquid brewed from parched rye, parched bits of sweet potatoes and other substitutes—was a poor substitute for "java" or "rio."

The early settlers brewed coffee in small pots with three short legs. The pots were placed on the coals in the wide fireplaces, and when water boiled, the coarsely ground coffee was dumped in and left to boil until the liquid was dark and strong. The small iron pots are antiques now, and the girls hunt them out and use them for planting flowers.

Then the big tin coffeepots with short spouts came in fashion when cookstoves were brought to homes to relieve housewives of the task of cooking on hearthstones. Before the war, the skilled ebony cooks in plantation out-kitchens knew the secret of brewing the most delicious coffee in the world in the little iron pots on the fireplace. Grandma said that coffee never tasted the same any more when brewed in a coffeepot on the stove.

After the war, coffee soon became plentiful, and the stores stocked big bags of green coffee beans. Grandma would take eggs to the country store to trade for green coffee, and it was a little girl's job to parch the coffee. It did no good to be told that the little servant girls parched the coffee in other years; we had to do that distasteful task now, and it was a chore.

Green beans in an iron skillet on top of the cookstove had to be carefully stirred around and around with a wooden paddle kept for this purpose. If we ceased stirring and the coffee burned, it would be just too bad. When Grandma pinched a dark brown bean and said, "It is done," that was a welcome relief. We don't remember why, but children seldom drank coffee then, and we wondered why adults just had to have so much coffee. It was a great day when Arbuckle Coffee came in packages with coupons for premiums. That was ground coffee, too, something new in the South. Heretofore, the parched coffee had to be ground in either the wall-type grinder nailed to the kitchen wall or the little square box-type grinder with the door in the side where you removed the ground coffee. Sabbath-keeping Scotch-Irish ground coffee on Saturday afternoon for Sunday morning coffee. Other mornings, the coffee was ground fresh for breakfast.

A hand-operated coffee grinder. *Artist Tommy Willis.*

The coffee was boiled in a tin coffeepot, and nobody thought it was harmful. If Grandma needed a coffee break, though she had never heard of the term, she poured an extra cup from the pot keeping warm on the back of the stove. Fire burned in the stove all day, and the coffeepot was never cold. Although children did not drink coffee regularly, Grandma thought no better food for a baby than a biscuit crumbled in a cup of coffee, rich with milk and sugar. The crumbled, softened biscuit with coffee was spooned into the youngster's eager mouth, and there were no pediatricians around to warn Grandma that coffee would harm the baby.

*Chapter 9*

# The Old Churn Dasher

Operation churn dasher was a chore dreaded by little girls in Grandma's day. It was a long, slow task to get the butter to come, and if you have no memories of working the dasher up and down, thump-thump, for hundreds of times before the flecks of golden butter began to form, you wouldn't know what we mean by "churning."

Much has been written about the matchless flavor of country butter, which went so well with fresh, hot bread, but no writer ever did justice to the monotony of working the churn dasher in a day when all household tasks were accomplished by elbow grease, not kilowatt power.

Down on the farm, the pails of frothy milk fresh from the cows were strained into an old-fashioned churn made of wooden staves bound by brass hoops, or in some homes, the churn was a large stone jar. The milk had to be "turned" before it was ready to be churned, and the business of scalding churns, pails and all utensils used in the process of turning milk into butter and buttermilk meant plenty of work for the housewife.

In summer, the heat turned fresh milk into clabber, but in winter, the churn with its contents was placed in a corner beside the fireplace, where it had to be frequently turned around to maintain the contents at an even temperature. A cozy picture—the old-fashioned churn, covered with a snowy white tea towel, in its place near the hearthstone. After the milk had been left overnight to "turn," Mother or Grandma would pronounce it ready to churn.

The dasher, a wooden crosspiece attached to a handle resembling a broomstick, would be scalded and placed in the churn. The handle fit the

Coleman demonstrates her grandmother's crockery churn in the 1950s. *Authors' family collection.*

opening of the churn's lid, and a cloth was tied around the lid to prevent splattering of the milk. In summer, the churning was done on a shady back porch, and a little girl assigned to the task of churning had to keep up a steady thump-thump, dash-dash, while other children played in the backyard. Cruelty to the little girl, who could hardly prevent mingling tears with the splashing milk. To the tune of "Come butter, come; the bread is waiting for you," the steady operation went on and on. At long last, Grandma would inspect the churn and say, "The butter is come"—never more welcome words. When the butter was taken up and worked into a golden mass, it was then molded in a wooden mold, which imprinted a floral or conventional design in the center of the top of the pound of butter. City cousins coming to the farm would rave over the pounds of butter. "Just think, you can have this delicious butter without paying for it!" And we would sigh at such ignorance of how that butter came.

The churn dasher was made by the home carpenter, or it might be stocked in the country store. You could trade a dozen eggs at the store for a new churn dasher that would last for years, despite the hard thumpings through many churnings.

Now that electricity has taken over the hard tasks once accomplished by elbow power, we do not even churn. We pick up butter at the supermarket, and the churn dasher is only an antique. We saw one not long ago in a junk shop, and a young woman exclaimed, "What in the world is that?" The very sight of the gadget brought back echoes of the dashing and thumping in the long ago.

## Chapter 10
# Foot Peddlers Brought
# "Riches of Araby" in Their Packs

The little weather-beaten foot peddlers who traveled the winding roads in Southern rural areas linked the remote countryside with the marts of trade. These picturesque peddlers were, for the most part, Italians, with a few Syrians and an occasional Irishman. All were foreigners; all were small men, stooped from the habitual bearing of heavy packs; all were lean and brown from exposure to the weather.

Even in the late Nineties, we recall the visits of the foot peddler bearing his pack, bringing the romance and glamor of faraway lands to rural homes. The peddler's pack was the dry goods shop, the notion counter to the Southern country home. That one small pack could hold so many varied stores was a puzzle explainable only by the peddler, whose skill in packing so much in so little space was acquired by long experience.

What a thrilling sight when we children playing in the yard would see a familiar stooped figure toiling up the lane. "Grandma, there's a peddler a-coming," we would call out as we hurried into the house.

Into the big living room the peddler would come upon Grandma's invitation. Unfastening the shoulder straps, he would lower his pack. Then, kneeling on the floor, he would unfasten the intricate knots in the worn black oilcloth covering, talking volubly all the while. We watched in wide-eyed wonder as the inner covering was unfastened and all the riches of Araby lay before us.

He would say, "I have nice goots, lady. Fine shawls, towels, tablecloths. Buy some lace for da leetle gurl. All da ladies buy my pillow shams."

Fervent exclamations were heard from the back of the room. Summoned by grapevine telegraph, every colored woman on the place had appeared to see the peddler's stock: fancy tuck combs, beads, sashes, creamy linen towels with red borders. What happiness when one of the "Aunties," untying her knotted kerchief, found that she had enough money to buy a towel or even a counterpane.

Pillow shams were the peddler's best sale, Nottingham lace shams lined with red calico to bring out the design of spreading peacocks. What grandeur such shams added to the company room bed!

It was a fine art to "trade" with the peddler, offering what he insisted was a "robbery price" for pillow shams or counterpanes. Invariably, he accepted the offer, which was what he had expected all the time.

Perhaps these Knights of the Pack had a sign such as a Romany Patteran to designate a good place for a night's lodging. Anyway, Grandma's home seemed to be favored by the peddlers. "Were you not afraid to take in that peddler for the night?" a neighbor would ask. Even on a cold, rainy night, the peddler might be refused a night's lodging at many homes because he was a foreigner, and it might be dangerous to admit him for a night.

It was thrilling to the children to hear a peddler, sitting by our fireside, tell of his home country in the great world beyond our doors—Italy, Spain, sunny France. Geography came to life by our fireside. And when one peddler told of the "Auld Countrie," Ireland, he found ready listeners who plied him with questions.

When the peddler asked for his bill the next morning, Grandma invariably refused any money. He never failed to bring forth from his pack a pair of beautiful linen towels or other articles. "A prisint, lady," he would say. Then shouldering his pack, he would set off along the road on another day's journey.

Time passed on, and fewer and fewer peddlers came to our doors. Finally, their visits ceased altogether, and another chapter in our saga of Southern rural life came to an end. It would be good to see just once more a little brown foot peddler with "nice goots" in his pack.

*Chapter 11*

# The Old Country Store

All over the country, there are more crossroads than ever before, but the old familiar country store that stood at the crossroads is gone. A modern service station now serves the travelers, but with the disappearance of the emporium known as the country store, a chapter in our rural saga came to an end.

A one-room frame building, long and low, the outside weathered to a soft gray, the country store building invariably had a small porch at the front. Here on warm days in the summer, the "country club" assembled to while away time and settle matters of the day. In winter, the "club" circled around the cast-iron, pot-bellied stove that burned wood and kept the store comfortably warm for customers. The club might center around a board of checkers, a favorite indoor sport, or it might engage in heated discussions of politics or the need for better laws. Many a matter of national import was settled by the country club without club members ever leaving the warm spot around the stove.

Shelves around the room were fronted by battered counters, scarred from long usage. Bolts of calico, denim, gingham and domestic were stacked on the shelves. Straw hats and horse collars hung on pegs above the shelves. Any article in use in that day could be found somewhere in the store. If not in sight on counter or shelves, the proprietor would search until it came to light. There were corsets, gloves, overalls, trace chains, lanterns, yards of lace and embroideries around the store, as well as needles and pins, buttons, overshoes, coffee grinders and hatpins.

In one corner stood the molasses barrel, and when a customer brought in a jug with a corncob stopper to be filled with molasses, the proprietor removed the bung, and the "glug, glug" sounded all over the store. In another corner stood a barrel of kerosene, and customers brought tin cans with potatoes stuck on the spouts for a supply of kerosene for lamps.

Grandma and her friends saved eggs until a box full had accumulated and then they took a basket of eggs to the store to trade for other commodities. "Yes, ma'am," the genial proprietor would say, "calico is seven cents a yard in trade, a little less in cash." Every needed article could be acquired in trade for eggs, and it was amazing to watch the figuring up of the amount of purchases in cash or trade. There were bottles of various patent remedies on the shelves; sulphur was sold in bulk, weighed out by the pound; Epsom salts were sold by the pound; castor oil came in huge bottles. If a horse collar was needed, one could be bought in trade. Coffee came in big bags, supplying the green beans that we took home and parched in the skillet and ground in the old coffee grinder. Calico was measured off with a yardstick, about seven yards for a dress, and the proprietor nearly always would say, "I'll throw in a few extra inches for good measure."

Before Christmas, there were coconuts and oranges, striped candy in boxes and raisins on stems in bunches. How wonderful when Grandma traded eggs for such glamorous things that we saw only at Christmas.

We would start back home with our purchases filling the back of the buggy. A trip abroad would not have been more wonderful than going to the country store. Not the grandest emporium in New York or other great cities can ever take the place of the old-time country store.

*Chapter 12*

# Day of the Button Shoe

If you were a little girl in the Nineties, your most cherished articles of apparel were your buttoned shoes. Life holds few happier moments and few greater thrills than a little girl experienced when she opened a shoebox brought from town and there found her first buttoned shoes.

Buttoned shoes were strictly for Sunday wear, and only for church on Sunday—nowhere else. On Sunday morning, little girls could hardly wait to put on the Sunday shoes and go switching around the house, stopping frequently to admire the shoes. Sometimes the children were taken to town and permitted to try on shoes, but we had to choose what Mother had chosen for us, and with no foolishness about being hard to please. We were allowed one pair of Sunday shoes, which we wore until they were outgrown, and then if there were any smaller sisters, the shoes were passed down. They were never worn out.

As soon as we returned from church, no matter how hard we might try to avoid Mother's notice, hoping that she would forget that we were wearing our buttoned shoes, we would hear the firm command, "Change your shoes before you come to the dinner table." How terrible the comedown, having to remove the wonderful and soft, comfortable shoes with shiny buttons, and don the heavier school shoes with laces or shoestrings instead of buttons. With what pride we had walked down the aisle at church feeling that every eye was looking at our new shoes with admiration—and now to have to put them away until next Sunday.

*Left*: Only one button, but big sisters had to help youngest. *From left to right*: Jean, Agnes and Margie Coleman in Sunday finery, 1916. *Authors' family collection.*

*Right*: Impish twins Broad and Bill (Broadus and William Coleman) wear button shoes, too. They were around age four in 1924. *Authors' family collection.*

There were no summer slippers nor sandals nor any of the contraptions of thongs and straps now called shoes. We wore the high-top, buttoned shoes summer and winter, until the styles began to change around the turn of the century, and "low cut" shoes or slippers became fashionable.

The buttoned shoes had tops of black cloth that fit snugly, and rows of buttons up the sides were bright and shiny. The shoes were buttoned up by means of a shoe button, and no implement in the house was more essential than the buttonhook. Sunday morning when we were dressing for church, the buttonhook had to be at hand. Could be that a careless little girl had lost the buttonhook that was not in its usual place, and if Mother learned that such was the case, it was too bad for the culprit. Usually, the gadget turned up before the entire household was disrupted, and all was well. However, a wire hairpin was often called into service, and buttons popped into place when a skilled hand manipulated the hairpin.

Buttons coming off our shoes caused minor troubles, and it was difficult to sew them on securely. If a little girl in a Scotch-Irish family failed to look to her shoes and sew on buttons on Saturday, she had to go to church on Sunday with a gaping buttonhole where a button ought to be. No sewing on buttons on the Sabbath Day was permitted, and after a little girl had suffered the humiliation of going to church with a button missing from her shoe one time, she was not apt to forget next time. Finally, the buttons were put on by the manufacturers with metal wire—bradded on—and there was no more sewing on of shoe buttons.

The ordinary buttonhook that came with the shoes, or which one purchased for a nickel, was a plain steel gadget several inches long, but there were more ornate buttonhooks for sale. Ladies who had beautiful toilet articles owned jeweled buttonhooks, and some were made of silver. We don't know what became of the old-time buttonhooks, but they might still be found in antique shops. Modern girls might like to carry the old-timers in their purses or hang them up in the living room just for "atmosphere."

## Chapter 13

# Waiting for "Second Table"

I f you have never had "company"—only "guests"—in the summertime, then you don't remember horse-and-buggy days when the good old summertime was the season for such visiting back and forth among kinfolks and neighbors, as the modern family knows nothing about.

All through the year, we expected to have company occasionally, but along in July, the visiting really got underway, and it lasted unabated until September.

The family then did not consist of parents and one or two children as now. There were nearly always a few little 'uns, young enough to go visiting along with the father and mother, and a few grown-up young people who did their own visiting without their parents. This added up to a lot of company in the summertime. And we children counted it pure joy when we could look up the road and recognize a familiar horse and buggy, with small faces peeping out and hands waving at us. There were more of our kinfolks coming to spend the day.

Grandma always knew just about when certain neighbors or kinfolks were due for a visit. She hadn't invited them for any certain day, of course. Such a thing was not done in that day, but friends simply took turns spending days, and you knew about when the time the Blankses' visit was due.

Unless you lived in that day, you will hardly believe it, but it's true that the surrey with the fringe or the buggy would make its appearance as early as 8:00 a.m. or half past, and the children would run shouting the news to Grandma. Mother or Grandma would hasten to spread the red-

Sprouse grandchildren wait for "second table" in 1917. *From left to right*: Jean, Mary Lou, Margie, Cecil, Kathleen, Lillian, Agnes and Alice. *Authors' family collection.*

checkered tablecloth on the dining room table. The fine white damask was kept for extra-special occasions, such as the preacher's visit, when we put on airs.

After welcoming the company, the children would get the table set, and then we were free to run and play until time to wield the fly brush while the elders ate.

Talking a blue streak all the while, the women, company and all, would go to the kitchen, don aprons and proceed with dinner. Families in rural areas lived at home, and company shared what we had. Vegetables had to be picked from the garden and prepared after company arrived. There was invariably an abundance of fruit in summer and yellow-legged frying chickens besides big country-cured hams in the smokehouse.

A typical dinner for spend-the-day company might include beans and potatoes, fresh corn, cucumbers, tomatoes, okra and squash; a platter of fried chicken, crisp and golden brown; a platter of ham, big tender pink slices; and always the chicken pie, oozing butter and cream. Then there were hot biscuits and cornbread, with coffee and buttermilk. Iced tea was not featured until the Naughts. Dessert would be damson or apple or peach cobbler. The food was all prepared after company arrived, and it was served from such china and glassware as you find only in collections of antiques today.

We children had to "wait" for the second table. There were so many grownups to occupy space around the first table, and they kept eating and talking until we despaired of ever getting anything to eat. How we peeped in at the door to watch the fried chicken, for fear it would all be eaten up. "The drumsticks are gone," one child would report in anguished tones to the waiting group in the yard. And the patient wielder of the fly brush would be ready to drop before the men began pushing back their chairs. Children of this age don't know what it is to wait and eat at the second table, but it was all a part of having company in the summertime in the Nineties.

## Chapter 14
# Home Remedies Down on the Farm

Concern about wolves was prevalent in the Nineties, and in our section, the wolves were not four-footed beasts of prey. They were little creatures that were found in lumps on the backs of the farmers' cows. But of trouble, they gave no end.

When the men looked out toward the pasture to see a fine cow cavorting around as if in distress, they said, "She has wolves on her back." Grandma had to hurry up and find the first-aid treatment for such hurt and ailing cows. A cow was not to be marked off as a loss until everything possible had been done to save her. The pesky wolves were lumps raised under the skin of the animal after a certain species of fly had laid eggs and managed to bury them under the skin.

*Dr. Chase's Remedies* told the family what to do, so Grandma opened the book at a well-thumbed page with a paragraph that said, "Wolves—and how to proceed when they infest your cows."

A pail of salt was taken to the cow barn, and with a coarse cloth, every animal's back was thoroughly rubbed with salt. Then they turned the animals loose to lick one another's back as they did their own disinfecting. The lumps, however, had to be first opened up with a sharp knife and the contents of lumps extracted.

There were no available experts on animal disease then, but in nearly every neighborhood, somebody knew what to do when there were ailing stock. If a cow moped and seemed listless and off her feed, the farm expert would first try the old tried and true cure for "hollow horn." Grandma, from

Veterinarian S.L. Coleman occasionally doctored his family with horse medicine. The horse with Sam, Agnes and Carrie, circa 1911. The homeplace is still on Fairview Street Extension, Fountain Inn. *Authors' family collection.*

long experience, pronounced the symptoms as "hollow horn, of course." One of the men would feel the horns; and if they were cold, he would bore into the horns with a gimlet. Then into the opening inject vinegar, pepper and salt. In case this didn't warm up the horns, the next thing to do was to take a couple of slices of salt pork, rub with cayenne pepper, and force the cow to chew on this.

However, if home remedies failed, they consulted *Dr. Chase's Remedies*. The good doctor explained that the above was good treatment for hollow horn, but a modern method was to dissolve an ounce of camphor gum in half a pint of alcohol, "pour half of it in one ear of the animal, and when it is done snorting and bawling, pour the other half in the other ear." We remember hearing that when hollow horn failed to yield to such treatment, the men just cut off the cow's horns. With no horns to be hollow, naturally the cow soon was chewing her cud and showing signs of good health.

As long as the family cow or the pastured cattle chewed their cuds, all seemed well on the farm. But let the favorite milk cow stand without chewing and there was cause for alarm. Unless she regained her cud, they had to call an expert, and in some cases the family doctor had to be called in. The standard treatment in such emergencies—and this, too, was recommended by Dr. Chase—consisted in making a new cud for the cow and poking it down her throat. Slices of salt pork rolled into a ball with a liberal dosing of cayenne pepper and additional salt were placed on Bossy's tongue. While strong men held her head, another man used a slim pole for poking down the cud until it settled in the proper location for cuds. Pretty soon, Bossy would be seen placidly chewing, and all was well in the barnyard.

## Chapter 15

# When Bustles Were in Style

There are some fashions that refuse to be permanently relegated to the past, and the bustle is chief among them.

Modern bustle fashions are but facsimiles of the genuine styles when the bustle was in its heyday, and no lady's street frock or other costume was complete without the bustle, which was the acme of fashion. The era of the bustle, as we remember it, was in the Gay Nineties and early Naughts, but long before that day, Southern belles wore bustles, as our mothers told us. When the beautiful hoopskirts of antebellum days were casualties of the blockade in the Sixties because the makings were no longer available, Southern ladies revived the fashion of the bustle from long-ago years. This ersatz gadget for adding style to an otherwise uninteresting costume became popular, and for years afterward, ladies felt undressed without their bustles.

The bustle played an important part in Southern history, though no monument ever perpetuated the memory of its service in the eventful days of the Sixties. Patriotic Southern girls, bravely acting as spies for the Confederate government, conveyed messages of import secreted in their bustles. A Southern lady with a pass to cross the lines on legitimate business might be suspected and searched, but she felt safe when papers were hidden in her bustle. No gentleman—not even a Yankee—would suspect a lady so far as to order that her bustle be searched.

Tintype pictures of young ladies of postwar days reveal that bustles—and large bustles, at that—were still in style. The items of the Gay Nineties were insignificant in size to those worn in earlier decades. One number hidden away in a chest for many years had a fine wire frame which had been covered with soft fabric; and when worn under the full skirts then in fashion, must have been distended to form almost a pillion in the back.

Around the turn of the century, the fashion was still going strong. Even street suits and frocks had to be worn over bustles. The full skirts, fitting neatly the slim waists in a day when waists were really kept slim, had to have slack enough below the waist to leave space for the bustle. The skirt fell gracefully to the floor or even into a small train, and somehow it looked just right with the bulge just below the waistline. Even the black silk or wool skirts with shirtwaists for best dresses and the filmy muslins and lawns worn to picnics and lawn parties were fashioned with short trains.

# Chapter 16

# Sassafras Tea

National "Take Tea and See Week" has for its purpose to promote the use of hot tea. Throughout the long, hot summer, Americans practically live on iced tea—Americans in the warmer areas, that is. Since the introduction of iced tea to supplant hot tea, Southerners have consumed comparatively very little hot tea.

A young girl who came from Ireland to make her home in the writer's Southern hometown had never heard of iced tea until she came here to live. On the Emerald Isle, hot tea for meals, especially afternoon tea and supper, was indispensable.

The custom of drinking hot tea was brought from the "Old Country" by our ancestors, and hot tea for meals in the warm South was not considered unsuitable even in the sweltering summers. Grandma said that her ancestors drank more tea than coffee, because in both Scotland and Ireland, tea was the favorite beverage. Quantities of tea brought to the colonies on early sailing ships sold readily to merchants and were carried to the remote areas, where all who had the price of tea bought it. It must have been a hardship when, after the Boston Tea Party, the cost of tea became almost prohibitive. For patriotic reasons, loyal colonists banned tea, and even in the homes of the rich, teas concocted from herbs were served with pride.

Southerners, especially those in the hill countries, soon learned to brew delicious tea from the roots of native sassafras. Possibly they learned this from the Indians, who taught the settlers how to use wild plants, roots and barks for many purposes.

After the Revolution, the coastal families were able to get all the imported teas they needed. Tea drinking was fashionable, and the rich used costly imported teas. Ordinarily, there were just two varieties, green tea and black tea, and it was customary when one ate in a public eating place for the waiter to ask, "Which kind of tea do you prefer?" meaning green or black tea.

A story told by Grandma concerned a resident of the southern hill country who went to Charleston to take a hogshead of tobacco grown on his farm. When he took his seat at a table in an inn, he ordered tea to accompany his meal. "What kind of tea, Sir?" the waiter asked. "Store tea," the man bawled out. "Do you think I come all the way to Charleston, to drink sassafac?"

"Sassafac" was a colloquialism for sassafras, and sassafras was the tea familiar to country people in the hills. Even after the Revolution, many people continued to drink sassafras tea for the sake of economy, and some drank it by preference. The spicy flavor and the delicious aroma made this tea irresistible. Grandma said that her people were so glad when they could again obtain the fine teas to which they had been accustomed in the Old Country. But with the outbreak of the War Between the States, imported tea was again contraband. Only as a few precious packages ran the blockade was there any tea in the South. But Southerners resumed the custom of sassafras tea without any complaining. Gracious ladies served sassafras tea from fine old tea services, and the amber brew that was poured into priceless china teacups was offered to guests without apologies.

Long after the war, even as late as the Nineties, nearly every housewife in the South dispatched a man or boy to the fields to dig sassafras roots from the bushes that grew in profusion around the edges of the fields. The leaves, stems and the dainty flowers of the plant gave off a delicious aromatic odor, but the roots were used for making tea. They were cut in small pieces, scrubbed and laid on shelves to dry. Just a few of the small roots were put in heavy teapots, let come to a boil and then steeped for a long time until the brew was amber or golden. Sassafras tea was supposed to have medicinal qualities. It would "thin the blood" and banish all "humors" from the blood.

## Chapter 17

# Passing of the "Amen Corner"

The "Amen Corner" was a familiar part of our church life in the past century. Unless you went to a country church in your childhood around the turn of the century, you never saw an "Amen Corner."

In the day when the little church was the center around which the entire neighborhood revolved, each church had its own custom of arranging the congregation's pews or benches. The smaller church buildings might have only one aisle, which divided the long benches on which the worshippers sat. And in such churches, it was an unwritten rule that the women sat on one side of the church and the men on the opposite side. The seats faced the pulpit, and on each side were several long benches facing the sides of the pulpit. One of these groups of seats up near the pulpit was designated the "Amen Corner." Here sat the elderly men, the "pillars of the church." The opposite group of seats was occupied mostly by elderly ladies, sometimes referred to as "Mothers in Israel."

The elderly men of the church were mostly the church leaders and officers, deacons, elders and stewards, according to the denomination of the church. As we remember, the term "Amen Corner" was more often used in the Methodist churches of that day, though we remember seeing such groups of men and hearing sometimes the "amens" in other churches in the country.

As children, we were impressed with the rapt attention these older brethren gave to the preacher's sermons. They would listen carefully, never taking their eyes off the preacher. Frequently, as the preacher made

Some Fairview Mothers in Israel and pillars of the church (from left to right): Lawrence Anderson, Molly McKittrick, Tempie McKittrick, Adeline McKittrick Simpson, Kitty McKittrick and Jeff McKittrick in 1927. *Authors' family collection.*

a telling point or brought out some forcible truth of the Scriptures, fervent "amens" would be heard from the occupants of the "Amen Corner." The loud or soft amens and the rapt attention evinced by the gentlemen made the "Amen Corner" seem like a very holy place. The pastor must have been encouraged and inspired by such cooperation from this particular group of worshippers.

The nice, elderly ladies who sat in the opposite corner were invariably clad in long, black silk frocks and matching "split bonnets"; sometimes they also wore black silk aprons. They were never heard to utter an "amen." Women, according to the Apostle Paul, "must keep silent in the church." But we could see their lips moving in silent approval of the sermon and their heads sometimes nodding in agreement of the amens from the opposite corner.

Church services had real meaning in that day. Members of the congregation calmly devoted themselves to the matter of worshipping, without thought of hurrying home before the final benediction was uttered. Nobody cooked on the Sabbath, anyway, and there was no use hurrying home to sit down to cold dinner. There was no such thing as having company or visiting on Sabbath. The horses would be turned out to pasture, and the family would spend the remainder of the day resting and meditating on the morning's sermon.

"Didn't you think Pastor Blank was very earnest this morning? And there were so many amens, too. We don't know when a sermon has called forth such hearty amens from over in the 'Amen Corner' as did that sermon today," the mother would say. And the father would review the sermon, relishing certain points and wondering about others, showing that the preacher really had listeners.

The "Amen Corner" went out of style with the passing of the century. Very few people now remember that there was such a sacred place in the country church away back when.

## Chapter 18

# Roof Covering

A roof covering was a cooperative affair in early days in the South, and still on some occasions, the cooperative "workings" were being held as late as the Nineties. The landowner would need a new roof on a barn or dwelling house, and since every man was his own carpenter, the neighbors would be invited to come and bring hammers.

Before the roof was to be covered, the shingles, then called "boards" (that is, if homegrown and split), had to be made ready. Board splitting was no light task. The landowner had to know which trees in the woodlands would make good roofing material, and he had his own methods of determining which trees to cut down. With heavy axes, he and his laborers would fell the trees, trim them up and cut them into proper lengths for boards. The whole thing was a matter of crude tools and elbow power.

The logs cut into lengths were evened by cutting off thin layers around the outer edges. Then a section was fastened tightly into crude bolts to hold the log fast. With a heavy maul made of the trunk of a hickory tree and a gadget known as a frow or wedge, the tree section would be split into blocks. With careful handling, the blocks were then split into boards or shingles of the required thickness.

The boards had to be "racked up" for drying out, for too green boards wouldn't make a good roof. The fragrance of freshly split boards was delightful, and we children would hang about at a safe distance when the board splitting was in progress. We were scolded if we came too near, for it sometimes happened that a board would split off and get out of bounds at the wrong time.

When the drying process was complete, the farmer sent word to his neighbors, and all came with hammers, wearing little aprons with pockets for nails. The best "roofers" would climb the ladder and go to work with hammer and nails, while other workers would pass up the boards. A clear day was selected for the "covering," for the old boards had to be removed and the interior of the house left exposed to the weather.

It was a merry din they kept up all day with hammers pounding in unison and all laughing and talking as they worked. A working was the time for passing jokes around and having fun.

Some of the nearest neighbors brought their wives along to help with the dinner. If it was a barn being covered, dinner was prepared in the home kitchen and served on long tables in the dining room. But when the residence had to have a new roof, it took a bit of doing to serve dinner to the workers.

Sometimes a stove would be set up in a shed near the house, and cooking utensils taken out to the shed. Big pots of beans, turnips or peas would be set to boiling in the yard, with one helper detailed to do the stirring and another

When built in 1858, this fourth Fairview Church building possibly had a shingled roof. It's still standing on Fairview Road, Fountain Inn. *Courtesy of Fairview Presbyterian Church.*

to keep the fires going. A big chunk of beef or several hens would be boiling in one pot, while pans of biscuits and cornbread, chicken pies and fruit pies baked in the oven of the stove in the shed.

Tables would be moved out to the yard and the goodly supply of food arranged for self-service. Men heaped their plates, and the women poured coffee from the big kettles, which had been steaming on a bed of coals. By the time all had eaten with much laughing and talking, and the dishes had been cleared away, the roof was finished.

When the last worker had departed, the family contemplated their snug, new roof with much satisfaction. Many hands made light labor at a time like that, and the spirit of neighborliness made warm hearts and happy homes.

*Chapter 19*

# Old Saturdays in Cotton Town

Cotton Town's Saturday night and its Saturday afternoon offer a study in America at this season of the year. But with the advent of the motor age, rural folks get into town more often, and the old Saturday holiday is not quite the festive occasion it once was.

September and October, when the cotton fields were white in horse-and-buggy days, were the busiest months of the year. No use to talk about going to town until Saturday, as the landlord, as well as the tenant and sharecropper, worked from daylight until dark, picking, hauling and weighing the cotton. By Saturday afternoon, every person was weary enough to drop. But they didn't drop in their tracks. All hurried through dinner and got ready to go to town.

Buggies or surreys were soon reaching town, and the horses were tethered to hitching posts along Main Street or in vacant lots. Cotton had been sold, and families had cash to purchase long-needed articles. Soon, the crowds were milling about the streets, entering the little stores, where mothers inspected clothing for their families.

One mother was purchasing material for frocks for her daughter, carefully testing the weave and color of material before spending her money. Another was outfitting her brood with shoes. Merchants and salespeople were busily trying to serve the customers. Rushing here and there, piling goods on counters, taking down shoes from the shelves, they eagerly sought to please. Now was the time when merchants make up for the dull months. Saturdays in cotton season are gold producing days.

The furniture store was a busy place, as ladies proudly selected a suit of furniture, a divan, a stove or chairs to be delivered when the wagon came to town. Even a few little luxuries might be purchased if the cotton was bringing a good price—beads for the little girls, roller skates and such. The landowner with a large cotton acreage had money to put in the bank when the cotton turned out well.

Toward night, the colored families were coming in and thronging the streets, eagerly enjoying the bit of holiday. Friends were exchanging greetings, and loud talk and laughter were heard. There was a spirit of good will and friendliness manifested, such as one likes to see.

The hot dog stands sent out a tantalizing aroma, and there was much eating going on. The grocery stores came in for plenty of the cash, as piles of fish and fresh meat were purchased along with the staples. We do not remember any misbehaving or any fighting going on about the streets. Salespeople were ready to drop by this time, but the crowd had thinned down; people were loading wagons or buggies and starting home. It would be a great day tomorrow when the family could start

The 1830s stagecoach stop and inn between Charleston, South Carolina, and Asheville, North Carolina. Its gushing spring inspired the name Fountain Inn for a cotton growing community. *Artist Art Frahm.*

out to church, all dressed up in new Sunday clothes or maybe riding in a new buggy.

A look at the crowds coming in to town in modern times is an eye-opener, if you remember earlier days. No buggies to be seen, no hitching posts to hitch the horses to—if you had any horses. Families come to town in cars that cost money and look like it. You seldom see a wagon. Still people throng the streets, not only on Saturday afternoons, but every afternoon in cotton time, and fall's "bright blue weather" is linked with cotton-picking time and the joys it brings.

## Chapter 20

# Day of the Traveling Dentist

B ack in the day of the traveling specialist in nearly every line, there was the traveling dentist who made the rounds of the rural sections, practicing his profession, with his implements under the buggy seat—all save the forceps, that is. The forceps, or "pullers," the most frequently used implement of his profession, usually reposed in the dentist's coat pocket. The handles of the pullers, plainly visible above his pocket, struck terror in to the hearts of all children.

Though we might be underfoot when the peddler stopped with his pack or the fruit tree salesman came with his big book of pictures, we remained out of sight while the dentist was on the place.

A beloved old dentist, Dr. Ball, pulled the teeth and made the dentures for two generations of patients in this part of the country. He traveled in a high buggy along the country roads, and he never hurried but jogged along at a leisurely pace, sure that his patients would be at home when he arrived. When Grandma could stand her aching teeth no longer, word was sent to Dr. Ball, and he promised to arrive at the home on a certain day—"God willing." Getting ready for the visit of the dentist savored of getting ready for the hangman. It was no joke to have dental work done in that day.

On the appointed day, we children saw the buggy coming down the road. We watched with interest as the doctor hitched his horse and, from the back of the buggy, removed some cumbersome equipment along with his long black satchel, very worn and shiny from use. With a cheerful greeting, the doctor would enter the house. About that time, we left. Who knew but that the doctor would say, "Open your mouth, and let's have a look?"

The patient would be seated in a kitchen chair, and a headrest was clamped to the chair back. The patient's head was clamped in the headrest, and rolling up his sleeves, the dentist was ready for business. We don't remember his sterilizing his instruments, but no doubt he did drop them in a dishpan of boiling water. No Novocain, no anesthetic of any kind was in favor then. It was the custom to offer the patient a stiff dose of whiskey, which was supposed to alleviate the pain and horror or else to make the patient so happy that no pain was felt. Grandma, being a stern Scotch-Irish Presbyterian, hated anything savoring of "spirits and strong drink," but even she was persuaded to take a few swallows of the drink, lest she fail to endure the ordeal.

The dentist calmly used his pullers in a mighty wrench and dropped the offending tooth into a basin. It seemed inhuman, but we remember that eleven teeth were once extracted at a sitting, with nothing save the few swallows of whiskey to deaden the pain. When the job was finished, the patient was about finished, too, but the dentist stayed on in the home to watch the patient, lest there be some after-effects. There were seldom any complaints; and after drinking plenty of strong coffee, the patient soon returned to normal. A good dinner on the table with big platters of country ham, fried chicken, potato pie, biscuits and coffee was waiting for the dentist when he had accomplished his mission.

He would promise to be along in about six months "to take the impression." Grandma gummed it for six months, and then along came the doctor to get the impression. After more weeks, he would come back with the "plates." Strange to say, we never knew anybody to complain of poorly fitting dentures. The good old doctor was a giant of his profession, and the old-timers thought it a sad day when the traveling dentist passed out of the picture. It was too much trouble to take a long buggy drive to town to the dentist's office, and who knew whether the young dentist knew his business, as did the old doctor?

*Chapter 21*

# When Grandma Laced

"Curves are back in fashion," a style report assures us. That means when next you stroll through the stores, a lovely siren will come smiling, saying, "You just MUST have a new foundation garment, or your new frocks will not look right!"

Feminine figures have had to conform to various shapes in the past—the string-bean shape, the curvaceous shape, long waist, high waist—and always there had to be the "foundation" to fit the shape to the styles.

Even the term "foundation" is new. Away back when, they were called "corsets" and not mentionable in polite society. They could have called them "torture," as that's what they were. Made of strong material and stout, unbendable whalebone encased an inch or two apart in vertical casings all around the whole garment, they might have well been made of plaster like a surgical cast. The whalebones were immovable, and the wearer was well nigh immovable as far as bending down was concerned.

Girls went to college encased in such contraptions and were never to appear out of their bedrooms without such garments. They wore them to picnics, to parties, everywhere, and it was the fashion to appear rigid and stiff.

We do not remember Scarlett O'Hara's day, when the young lady tied the foundation strings to a bedpost and pulled until she could barely draw a breath, and then stepped out with knotted strings confining her twenty-two-inch waist, a fashionable gown swirling about her. But Mother told me that girls of that day really "laced," as it was called, until they could barely eat a bite or so of food when dressed for a company dinner.

In the Naughts, girls were wearing snappy numbers, whalebone-encased high above the waist, tapering down to a midget waist and stopping off a few inches below the waist. The hourglass figure was in fashion, and just a bit of "lacing" was required to make the whalebone do its job of confining an hourglass figure. Wide, full skirts were in fashion, swirling out from the small waist. When spending the day, if a girl ate more than a few morsels of food, it was misery to sit around in the whalebone corset.

Another style later was the dropped waistline. Down almost to the knees it dropped, and manufacturers were right on the job, getting the ladies

Fairview women laced and wore corsets until the 1950s. Carrie Coleman, age twenty-six, with infant Agnes in christening gown, is seen in this photo, circa 1908. *Authors' family collection.*

into straight, stiff foundations, making the lines conform to fashion rather than leaving them where nature had intended.

Back came the waistline to where the waist is meant to be, and then came the elastic girdles. Girls just stepped in and kept wriggling around until they were enclosed, waistline in place. Now, they could whisk around in freedom with no instrument of torture to hinder their progress.

Then they sought still more freedom. The girls shed their girdles and went around looking as nature made them. If one looked like a meal bag tied with a string and another like a fence rail, it didn't seem to worry them. "Just think, those old-timers used to wear girdles," the dears kept saying. But that style couldn't last. It takes manufacturers to put curves where they should be and to place the waistline where fashion demands. And how were the manufacturers to live and pay income tax if the girls refused to let figures be conformed to fashion? So they went back to girdles, and not just any old girdle at that: a little number as light as foam, with a silken, soft texture and that famed "two-way stretch."

Now that was something. See the graceful wearers tripping along the street, walking on air, as it were. And see in the museums the various styles in foundations from great-grandmothers' whalebones to great-granddaughters' thistledown stretch. It's a long trail between the numbers, a trail with the whitened bones (whalebones, that is) of the old-timers and with the moldering remains of girdles—high-waisted, drop-waisted, laced and hooked or stepped into—that kept the ladies in fashion's figure through the years.

## Chapter 22

# The "Big Ha Bible"

Who has not found inspiration in Robert Burns's "The Cotter's Saturday Night," especially in his description of the "Big Ha Bible" as read to the family circle at evening time?

Just such memories of reading the family Bible around the fireside linger in the minds of many older people who were reared in the traditions of a Scotch-Irish ancestry.

In the rural homes in the little Scotch-Irish communities where we grew up, the big family Bible was the center around which family life revolved. The big Bible was kept on a round table in one corner of the living room by the fireplace. That little Bible stand of other years is now an antique, and replicas are sold in all good furniture stores. A sight of the familiar table paints a picture in my mind: a large, low-ceiled living room, with priceless oak or walnut paneling, the high chest of drawers, the bookcases, settee, rocking chairs and the big chair beside the Bible stand.

After supper, the family assembled in the living room, and while the women busied with sewing or knitting, the men looked over the papers and talked of the crops. Soon it would be bedtime. Fresh lightwood knots would be thrown on the fire, and the father or grandfather would pick up the Bible. Then, with the soft firelight flickering on youthful faces in the family circle, he would read slowly and with feeling a chosen passage from the Word. The Bible would be reverently placed in its place on the stand, and all would kneel in prayer.

Mary Ann Stennis, "Grandma" McKittrick, about seventy years old, is seen with the "Big Ha (Hall) Bible" beside her against a woven counterpane coverlet background, circa 1895. *Authors' family collection.*

In such a home with such traditions, there was no problem of juvenile delinquency. There were fewer divided homes, and such a thing as "nervous breakdowns" was almost unknown. The "Big Ha Bible" was, in many cases, the same Bible brought over from the Auld Countrie. The pioneers could bring but few of their possessions in the crowded boats, but the Bible was not left behind. It had reposed on a Bible stand in the stone cottages of Scotland and Ireland. On its pages were recorded births: "In County Antrim" or "Born on the River Ayr," and "Died at – America" would be the inscription to follow in many of the records.

The record went on through succeeding generations, and most historical societies now accept family Bible records as indisputable proof of births and marriage, which were recorded also on blank leaves for the purpose. On Sunday afternoons, the children liked to read the inscriptions on the white pages of the Bible, unconsciously acquiring knowledge of family history.

The Bible was the pioneers' filing case. Clippings of interest, especially obituaries, were placed between its pages. Great Aunt Elizabeth's recipe for pound cake and grandfather's method of curing hams, time-stained and torn, were somewhere in the Bible. You could find a pair of spectacles—lost but kept safe in the Bible. Not without a sense of dry humor, some people secreted money in the Bible. Thieves will never look in the Bible, it was thought.

Now there are Bibles by the tons, in formats to meet every person's needs, but the "Big Ha Bible" no longer occupies its place as the center of the American home. Not long ago, we saw a fine old family Bible lying dusty in a secondhand furniture shop, and we wondered what we would find if we could follow up that family with the Bible gone from the home.

*Chapter 23*

# Cotton-Picking Time in Dixie

gain, it is cotton-picking time in Dixie. Older people who recall the "Good Old Days" when cotton was king in the South have twinges of nostalgia as they view the changed landscape in modern times. Where once was a sea of white over broad acres and rolling fields as far as the eye could see now are much smaller fields alternating with fields of weeds or so-called cover crops, partly smothered with native grasses.

Yet despite the decreased acreage, cotton is still a staple crop in this area; and the pickers are now in the fields while trucks are speeding from the ginnery to the farms, to pick up the raw cotton and convey it to the gin. This is the highlight of the year in the cotton belt.

In the old days, farm life in the South revolved around cotton. There was the planting in spring, as well as fertilizing and cultivating, until laying-by time about the first of August, and then in early fall, the picking and ginning began. Could be that picking and ginning continued until nearly Christmas. Even on Christmas Eve, we might see the last of the open bolls being picked and wagons loaded with the weather-stained cotton on the way to the gin. There were no boll weevils then to ruin the last bolls, and bolls would mature and open even in cold weather.

October was the prime month for cotton picking, and all had to be made ready before the first of September, as sometimes cotton began opening early. Big baskets were made ready, and all fertilizer bags on the place were washed and dried, ready for use as pick sacks. The colored people invented a method for making picksacks. Each picker made ready a broad strap. He turned back the top of a fertilizer sack several inches from the top. In each corner of the sack, he inserted a green cotton boll, then fastened the cloth and boll by tying a knot with the strap after adjusting the strap to the length needed to bring the picksack up to his waist or a little below. Easing along between two rows of cotton, the sack continually growing heavier with its load of cotton, the cotton picker usually kept things lively by occasional snatches of song.

The task was made easier if several were working in the field together. Nothing could be more indicative of life in Dixie than the scene in a cotton field—rows of pickers bending in unison, straightening up to thrust big handfuls of fleecy cotton into the brown picksacks and bending again. Sometimes all would sing together, the rhythm of their movements seeming to keep time with the tunes—usually a sad, plaintive melody sung in inimitable fashion of the ancestors of the singers, and sometimes the pickers only hummed the tunes.

A wagon was driven to the field, and the cotton was weighed on the "steelyards" at the end of the day and then emptied into the wagon ready for the gin. Cotton pickers gathered around watching the weighing made a scene worthy of an artist's brush. "Cap'n" weighed the individual baskets and passed out to each picker his or her share, "paid by the hundred pounds."

Big gourds or jugs of water were placed in the shade, and in cooler weather, the pickers each brought a "snack"—baked potatoes or hunks of bread—to the field to save time, and all would sit around the container of water, eating and drinking, swapping jokes. After weighing was over, all proceeded toward their homes, where smoke would soon be rising, along with the fragrance of baking corn pones drifting out to scent the atmosphere.

*Chapter 24*

# Hog-Killing Time on the Farm

Good hog-killing time" in the Piedmont meant work for everybody on the farm. Farmers were weather-wise, and along in early December, the weather was due to get right for hog killing.

When a cold, clear night in early winter presaged hog-killing weather, the preparations were begun. The colored men piled up plenty of wood ready for starting fires, with a big basket of chips nearby. A big sack of salt was ready in the meat house. Grandma got her sausage seasonings ready.

Long before the sun was up, the men were out in the barnyard making sure that the weather was favorable. A coating of ice on the horse trough and clear skies meant that this was the day. Provided, that is, that the signs were right and it was the right time of the moon. The "Cap'n" might scoff at the suggestion of killing hogs by the moon and the signs, but no self-respecting laborer would disregard such important portents as the dark and light of the moon or the signs in the almanac.

All things favorable, the big iron pot was set on the fire that the men were kindling out at the wash place. While some went to dispatch the two big hogs, others tended the fire and stood around warming themselves and laughing and joking. There was always fun at hog-killing time, as old-timers exchanged reminiscences about cold weather and big hogs away back when. There was hot water in the big hogshead, and the carcass of the slaughtered hog was soused into the water.

Soon the big, clean carcass would be hoisted by a pulley onto a limb of a tree or a cross piece between two posts, and a skilled craftsman would get the business of dressing the interior of the carcass out of the way.

On a stout table, the meat would be cut up into hams and shoulders, neatly trimmed; great slabs of "middling"; and big tubfuls of makings for sausage and lard. The head and liver were to go into liver pudding; the feet carefully cleaned and scraped would make the tasty dishes of fried pigs' feet and, lastly, the "chitlings" were eagerly taken over by the colored women, who would enjoy that rare delicacy.

After the meat had been cut up, big tubs of fat and lean trimmings were brought into the kitchen. Grandma and her helpers went to work getting the sausage ground. The old-fashioned sausage grinder was screwed down to a bench, and the one who turned the grinder sat on one end of the bench while another person fed the meat into the grinder. There was the art of seasoning the sausage with black pepper, home-grown and home-ground cayenne pepper, which was not ground so fine, but flakes of the red liberally added color to the sausage; also home-grown sage, dried through the summer and pulverized by rubbing the dried sage leaves between the hands. A quantity of sausage was set aside for immediate use, and there were several "messes" for the neighbors who would send us messes of sausage when their hogs were killed.

The remainder was put into muslin bags, smoothed down and left out overnight to get firm and frozen, and then hung from the rafters of the smokehouse or meat house to keep all winter and into spring. If you never ate sausage dried in this way, you have missed a tasty treat.

One of the helpers was expert at "rendering" lard, and she sat beside the big iron pot that boiled at the kitchen hearthstone, busily stirring the meat until the cracklings were crisp and brown. Lard was strained into big stone jars, and the brown cracklings went into many a pone of crackling bread like nothing else in this world.

Liver, head and trimmings went into liver pudding such as no cook could make unless she had the art passed down from an old-timer.

*Chapter 25*

# Old-Time Corn Shuckings

Come to the Blanks Friday night to a corn shucking" the word would go out over the neighborhood in the Nineties. Moonlit nights in early fall were just right for corn shuckings. Farmers gathered in their corn and piled it in huge piles on the ground in front of the corncrib. Then the neighbors would cooperate in a corn shucking, at various homes until all the corn had been stored in cribs before cold weather set in.

The corn shucking was the last of the cooperative "workings" established by early settlers to go out of fashion. As late as the late Nineties, the neighbors in our section were still gathering for corn shuckings.

We children could hardly wait for the time to come. Before sundown, the men would be coming with lanterns in their hands, and all would take seats around the big pile of corn. The colored men liked to come to corn shuckings too, for the fun and the good supper. All around the corn pile there would be laughter as one after another joked and teased. From the side of the corn pile where the colored men were grouped came the loudest laughter of all. A steady thump, thump as the shucked ears of corn were thrown into the crib kept time to the fun.

Some of the wives of the shuckers had been invited to come along to help prepare supper, and the colored women on the place were busy at work. We children could hardly stay out of the kitchen, where tantalizing odors made us ravenous.

When all the corn had been shucked, the men were called to supper, and they trooped into the house "just starving," as they said. On the long table in the dining room, there would be a feast spread. Huge pans of chicken pie such as only old-time cooks could prepare, along with platters of roast beef, platters of country ham, spare ribs and back bones. There would be bowls of turnips and greens, sweet potatoes baked and candied, dried fruit pies, potato pies, pound cake and plenty of buttermilk and coffee for many helpings.

On another long table on the back porch where the colored men sat to eat and talk and laugh, the same food was served to them, and they were glad to come to the shuckings just to eat all they could hold of such wonderful food.

We children hung around watching the men eating and wondering if any food would be left. But there was always enough left to last for a day or two. Sometimes a whole chicken pie would be left over, and that delicacy warmed over for breakfast was the greatest treat we ever had.

Finally, the men would light their lanterns and start walking home across the fields or through the woods. In a few more days, another neighbor would send out bids to a corn shucking and so on until they had gone the rounds.

*Chapter 26*

# Christmas in the Nineties

Plank guns booming, firecrackers popping, wood fires roaring up the chimneys, snow on the ground, the fragrance of cedar and holly all through the house and happy colored friends calling out, "Chrismas gif"—that was Christmas in the Nineties.

For days before Christmas, an atmosphere of mystery enveloped the place. We children searched for hidden packages, just for the thrill of feeling the outside of a package and trying to guess what it contained.

When the grown-ups returned from town with paper-wrapped bundles in the back of the buggy, they would tell us to stay away from the buggy, and after we were supposed to be asleep, the bundles would be brought in the house and carefully hidden—all most mysterious and glamorous, a part of getting ready for Christmas.

We never failed to hear, "Santa Claus is poor this year, and he won't have enough things for all the children in the world." Still, with magnificent faith, each child would borrow one of Grandma's large home-knit stockings and hang it before the fireplace on Christmas Eve.

We hurried off to bed soon after supper, lest Santa Claus come and catch us still awake and pass by our chimney without coming down. "Put out the fire," we would plead as we trooped up the stairs. How dreadful the thought of a hot fire when Santa Claus was expected to slide down the chimney.

Too excited to sleep, we were awake before daybreak and whispering to each other. Then the sound of plank guns would let us know that our neighbors were up, and we could stand it no longer. We would rush

Snow and oak picket fence surround 1899 Homeplace of Sprouse, Stewart and great-great-granddaughter Kristan Garrett/Thomas Tripp. Fairview Road, Fountain Inn. *Drawing by Skip Shelton.*

downstairs, and our shrieks of joy when we saw the filled stockings would rouse the house. There were continual squeals as we emptied stockings and examined the contents. For each child, there would be rosy red apples, sticks of striped candy, a few raisins—what joy, raisins! Only at Christmas—then a few nuts and the crowning glory: a big golden orange. Poor little rich children of modern times; with all you have, you are still underprivileged. Never to know the joy of having just one orange a year—the Christmas orange—ambrosia and nectar couldn't compare with its taste.

For each child, one gift: a little boy would have a knife, or cap-pistol, or a ball, and there would be little packets of firecrackers. For each little girl, a china doll, with a frock made by Mrs. Santa, or a little tea set. What visions of doll tea parties the sight of a tea set would bring. Once in a lifetime, a little girl would get a wax doll, just too wonderful to be true. Sometimes there would be china cups with floral designs and mottoes in golden letters: "Love the Giver," "Forget Me Not" or "For a Good Girl."

Cherished by the little girls, these "Christmas cups" would be kept for years—if there were no small brothers and sisters with clutching hands.

Mrs. Robert Quillen, wife of the late writer-humorist, had a collection of genuine "Christmas cups." The items are very hard to find.

Soon, we would join the boys who were gathered around a shovel full of glowing coals carried from the fireplace to the backyard and would be shooting their little firecrackers. In the meantime, plank guns were heard all over the neighborhood.

It was difficult to get the excited children to eat breakfast, such a country breakfast—ham and eggs, sausage, grits, hot biscuits, jam and jelly. The colored people would peep in at the door, each trying to "get your Chrismas gif," and there was always something for each one.

Soon the kinfolks would be driving up in buggies and carriages, with hot bricks at their feet and warm lap robes tucked around them, calling out greetings.

All would sit down to a groaning dinner table, with ham and turkey or baked chicken, country-killed beef, sausage and spare ribs, homegrown vegetables, pies and cakes of every description and always tall stemmed goblets of golden boiled custard—standard Christmas dessert.

This was just the beginning. All through the week, we visited from house to house, and "big dinners" were nearly the same everywhere we went—costing almost nothing in cash—for the food was grown at home, save for the coffee and sugar bought with the eggs at the store.

*Chapter 27*

# The Old-Fashioned Garden

A GARDEN is a lovesome thing, God wot"—and a garden does not have to be a scene of rare and costly plants, a plot on which money has been lavished and expert landscape artists have worked out intricate plans. Gardens in the Piedmont in the past century had a beauty and charm of their own, quite apart from the famed gardens on the coast. Lowcountry gardens have always had their charm, and in early years, our ancestresses here in the Upcountry were wise enough to know that they could not duplicate Lowcountry plantings, but they could and did create beauty with native plants.

In antebellum days, the South Carolina Upcountry had outgrown its "backcountry" aspect, so styled by the aristocrats of the coastal settlements. Plantations were not so vast as those established in the Lowcountry, but they had broad acres, fertile soil and great forests in the background. The planters built new homes to replace the outmoded pioneer dwellings, and each plantation mistress and each small farmer's wife was eager to make her premises a scene of beauty. Records and descriptions of the old gardens in the Piedmont have been passed down from generation to generation, and it seems that one might restore such an old garden, which would recall memories of a happy past.

In Lower Greenville County, in a community remote from the towns and cities, descendants of the pioneers built substantial antebellum homes, and the gardens created by loving hands were still flourishing long after the war. The invading armies had bypassed this section, but a war-impoverished people, short of labor, had to stint on caring for their gardens.

Yet as late as the Nineties, the old-fashioned gardens still held much of their former interest. The gardeners of that day depended largely on cuttings to keep their stock of plants from dying out. As we remember, nearly every plant in Grandma's garden was either a hardy survivor of the golden era before the war or had been obtained through exchanging cuttings or seeds with a neighbor.

There were many tall oak trees around the place, but at one side and in the rear of the house, there were sunny spots where flowers grew. Such flowers as marigold, Johnny-jump-ups, Jacob's ladder, princess feather, zinnias and hardy chrysanthemums, then called "pinks," grew in profusion along the borders and even in the kitchen gardens along the narrow walks. Spice pinks filled the air with sweetness after rains

"Mattie" Martha Jane McKittrick Sprouse, about sixty-five, smiling in the front yard garden of her Sprouse/Stewart home, circa 1920. *Authors' family collection.*

in summer, and in spring, there were thousands of old-fashioned daffodils, jonquils, butter 'n' eggs, snowdrops, hyacinths and blue iris, called "flags," all around the place.

Tall lilacs and great clumps of "Easter roses" grew against the garden fence. There were the old-fashioned velvet roses, the beautiful Paul Neyron and many others that we sometimes still find blooming in old gardens. A white running rose with slender pointed buds and very thorny foliage was a favorite among the neighbors, and this rose dated back to the pioneers. Great boxwoods bordered all the front walks, and they, too, had a history. Little twigs had been brought from the old country and planted out in the rich soil in the forests of Greenville County. In later years, many of these old-time favorites were discarded by modern gardeners who wanted to be in the fashion with privet hedges.

Crepe myrtle grew into tall trees, and these were indestructible. Cut down a tree, and the old stump would send up new shoots. There are still growing around old home sites, where even the foundation of the home is gone, sturdy crepe myrtles produced on aged stumps. One invariable feature was the ivy tree. Ivy planted at the base of a tall tree gradually climbed to the top and took over the tree. No old home was without its ivy tree. There was a well in every yard with its roof and its picturesque well sweep, "a modern convenience" that replaced the spring. But the old springhouse was kept in good order for cooling purposes. Around my grandmother's wide yard was a fence of oaken palings. One almost exactly like it now surrounds the "Little White House" at Warm Springs, Georgia. The carriage drive was just outside the fence. One walked down the wide sanded walk between boxwood borders to the front gate, which opened on the carriage drive. Nearby were the hitching posts so essential in that day.

Poets sing of the great gardens of the Lowcountry, but here in the Piedmont, we have right to be proud of our gardens, too.

## Chapter 28

# The Straw Broom

"You can judge a housekeeper by looking at her broom" was an old saying. You have to be able to remember the day of the old straw broom in order to understand the meaning of that saying. It took a bit of doing to care for the old-fashioned straw broom, to keep it neat and tidy instead of lopsided and frowzy looking, with the end of its broom string coming loose. The whole house appeared untidy if the broom was unkempt in appearance.

If you remember that long-ago day, you recall that brooms were made in midwinter. A supply to last several months would be made up and carefully stored in the smokehouse or the old out-kitchen. Broom straw was cut in November after early frosts and before a hard freeze, which would injure the quality of the straw and cause the stems to be too brittle.

Broom sedge grew all along the old fields and hedgerows, wherever there were uncultivated spots. The tall, fine broom straw grew on good fertile land, while poor land was recognized by stubby straw or broom sedge. In lower Greenville County, land near the Reedy River was rich, and the soil produced extra-good broom straw.

When the time came for cutting straw for brooms, we children were allowed to go with the colored "Aunties" on a broom straw expedition. Each adult carried a sharp knife, and they knew where the best crop of broom sedge was to be found. Across the creek and through a big woods we went to the New Ground, where the straw grew so tall and so thick that only a short time was required for cutting as much as all of us could carry. The fuzz on the straw kept us sneezing, but we would manage to get back home with the piles of straw.

The women took kitchen forks and combed the straw to take out the fuzz and then laid the cleaned straw in piles in a dry place in the storeroom or smokehouse to "season." About the middle of January, when the supply of brooms had given out, Grandma started making brooms. She would take enough straw for one broom, a "hand" she called it, and work with a fork again to get out the last of the fuzz. When she had enough "hands" laid in separate piles to make as many brooms as she wanted, she started tying the brooms. She had broom strings ready at hand.

The old-fashioned cord known as broom string was made on the same principle as a rope. Grandma took cotton thread and stretched two long strands out four times as long as the string was to be, then doubled back the strands and started twisting. A little girl held one end of the string, and Grandma held the other. Each began to twist in opposite directions until the length of strings was well twisted, and then letting one end loose from the middle of its length, the entire length would twist itself into a larger string, which tied in a knot at the ends made a miniature rope.

It was an art to make a broom string, comparable to the making of rope at the naval ropewalks, but more of an art to the tying of a broom. When the broom was complete, the string had been wound around the upper part of the straws, which were bunched together, down past the central length of the broom. Here the string was tightly wound and the ends of the straw branched out to form the brush of the broom with the upper part as the handle. The string had to be tightly secured at the top, and occasionally one had to partly rewind the broom to tighten the string. It was a pleasure to pick up a broom with string taut and every straw in place, but a disgusting thing to have a sloppy broom coming apart as it was handled. Floors looked clean when swept with good straw brooms, but modern housewives would think it long, slow work. The saying "A new broom sweeps clean" refers to the newly made straw broom, which could be swished over the floors, under the beds and furniture with a minimum of effort.

## Chapter 29

# The Fly Brush

"Now, whatever in the world is that thing?" was asked by one of the modern youngsters recently when a woman made a replica of the old-time fly brush and took it to a picnic where it was obviously needed.

A generation or two has grown up since the heyday of the old newspaper fly brush of pre-screen days. Not until after the turn of the century were window and door screens in vogue. There were then no machines spraying the fields with pest killers and thus helping with the housefly problem. How did we manage back in the not-so-good old days when swarms of flies flew in at doors and windows, settling over any uncovered food and swarming around the baby's cradle?

Somehow, we just kept fighting but never winning the battle. There was Tanglefoot, the sticky paper that we placed at strategic points about the house, and when well loaded with unwary flies, there was no more detestable sight. Then a black paper supposed to be coated with deadly insect poison was placed in saucers, moistened and set out to tempt flies to drink. Or we sometimes used various insect powder, sprinkling the powder around and then closing the rooms. All these methods only helped to keep the pests from getting worse but did not get rid of the swarms.

When we sat down to eat, we had to have the fly brush at hand or else fight flies as we ate. The brush, a familiar gadget in every home, was made by cutting a length of smooth cane about four feet long. Over part of the cane at one end, we hung several thicknesses of newspaper, much as the papers are hung on little rods in the libraries.

The papers were cut at the bottom, making the brush about ten inches deep. Then, with large needle and strong thread, the papers were sewn tightly to the cane or rod. Next, we cut the papers in slits with the scissors. The strips were about two inches wide, and the slits were cut from the bottom almost to where the papers were attached to the rod. Then we pleated or crinkled the strips to make a frilly brush, with the long part of the rod as the handle. When this contraption was waved gracefully back and forth over the table, flies kept their distance.

When company came in summer, a little girl had to stand at attention beside the dining room table and wield the fly brush. Adults just ate and ate, and the brush-waving tired small arms, but still the waving had to be kept on. Sometimes a little girl would let the brush dip into the gravy, and without knowing it, she would whish the brush on its arc, right into the face of a guest. Red-faced with embarrassment, the youngster would want to turn and run, but such was her training that she stood steadily in her place.

Some families saved the pink tissue paper that came in boxes with Sunday shoes and made fine fly brushes for use only when company came, the last word in style. When no company was with us, we all sat down at the table, and we took turns at waving the fly brush. At picnics, we just broke off long branches from a bush and used them as makeshift fly brushes. Who would have thought that the time would come when the sight of a fly brush would elicit such a query, "What in the world is that thing?"

## Chapter 30

# The Split Bonnets Were Enduring

I t's a sign of a hard winter when the girls begin to tie up their heads in rags," some wit has said. This recalls that, while every style in headdress from Empress Eugenie down to our "black Mammy's headrag" of slavery times has been revived, the girls have failed to bring back the "split bonnet" of our great-grandmother's day.

Recently, a Southern novelist's mention of "split bonnets" caused a mild controversy. "It's not split—it's slat," said one, while another stood up for "splint" as the correct usage. In the Piedmont, the split bonnet was worn by pioneer women to meeting on Sundays.

Even in this part of the South, when life was beginning in the Piedmont, and for years afterward, the split bonnet was worn by pioneer women. The Scotch-Irish who came down the Catawba path to settle the South Carolina Upcountry had first settled in Pennsylvania or Virginia. They may have borrowed the fashion from the thrifty women of Pennsylvania, or they may have brought it from the Old Country, but here in this section, they wore the bonnet that is immortalized by the statue of the "pioneer woman" famed all over America.

Later, when men of the Piedmont were growing cotton and making annual trips to Hamburg to market, they would bring back supplies from market, and these sometimes included "finery" for the women. The writer's grandmother, a little girl in the 1830s, was happy when her father brought back from Hamburg a quilted satin bonnet for his daughter, "fit for a queen to wear."

Girls now began to acquire silk or satin bonnets for Sunday best, while they wore bonnets of sprigged muslin trimmed with ribbon bows for other wear. Still, the older women clung to their split bonnets. "And what will you do about riding horseback without a split bonnet to keep the sun from freckling your face?" a mother would admonish her daughter.

During the Sixties, even many of the older matrons were wearing bonnets of black straw, poke bonnet shape, and forty years later, they were still wearing the same bonnets to church. By that time, the straw had assumed a patina of age that new ribbons couldn't hide. Still, some of the old-timers clung to the silken split bonnets—they didn't want to appear "uppity" in straw bonnets.

Not all the old split bonnets had gone into discard in the Nineties. They could be seen on some of the sweet-faced old ladies sitting in an old country church, in a corner facing the pulpit—and wearing their black silk bonnets.

Granddaughter may have been red-faced with embarrassment when Grandma went down the church aisle bobbing her bonnet, but no amount of pleading induced Grandma to don a stylish straw.

They saved cigar boxes to make the "splits" or used cardboard strips, inserting these in casings left when making the bonnet. A ruffle to frame the face was added. A flat crown was sewed to a gathered ruffle, which was long enough to reach the shoulders, forming the tail of the bonnet. Strings of the material to tie under the chin were affixed, and then Grandma was all set with a Sunday bonnet for the next twenty years. She only wore it to church services or funerals; there was the calico or homespun bonnet for other wear, and all had splits.

The splits could be removed to launder the bonnet, making the bonnet very practical and just the thing for riding horseback. With the strings tied under the chin, the face was protected from sun and wind. In fact, the face was so completely hidden by the split bonnet that the girls were glad of the new styles.

What use to rub the cheeks with mullein leaves to make them rosy only to have them hidden by the old bonnet?

*Chapter 31*

# Avoid Water during "Dog Days"

The ancient Egyptians were right in their belief about "Dog Days." There would be plenty of rain when Dog Days began, and the Nile would be flooded to give life to the crops. We are now in the midst of the annual season once called "Dog Days," and it seems that the old-time prophecy concerning rain on the first day of Dog Days meant rain for forty days. We are going right along with our forty days and nights of rain, and it could be that there will be no cessation of showers and downpours until the season wanes.

There has never been complete agreement concerning the regular time for Dog Days' beginning. The Egyptians, it was said, counted forty days from the time they saw Sirius, the Dog Star, rising. The Romans would have it that when the Dog Star rose at the same time of the sun's rising, the hottest weather of the summer had begun and so came the term "Dog Days." The English counted St. Swithin's Day, July 15, as the first of the Dog Days. If it rained on St. Swithin's Day, it would rain for forty days, and there was much watching of the clouds as this important day approached.

Whether or not our ancestors brought this superstition from the Old Country, they placed a great deal of faith in the sayings about what to do and not to do on Dog Days. "Be careful, this is Dog Days season," they would admonish children when children went out to play. A stray dog means danger in this season, and children were to avoid any dog unknown to them. Even the family dog might offer a menace, and we carefully watched Rover for any signs of foaming at the mouth or other abnormal symptoms that might indicate madness. Dogs were supposed to suddenly go mad during the season, and with signs of madness, they would take to the road to snap at any passerby. We had to hunt up the "madstone" to have it handy in case of any bite from a dog, not that we ever got near enough a stray canine to risk a bite.

Either too hot or too dry or too rainy for forty days, the weather was to be reckoned with. In spite of much rain, water was to be avoided. If a boy had a sore on his foot or a stubbed toe, he did not dare go in the old swimming hole during Dog Days. The sore would not heal until the end of the forty days if exposed to water. It was a good excuse for the youngster who hated to wash his feet at night, but a sad thing when other boys went swimming, and the one afflicted with a sore foot had to sit on the bank and watch out for dogs. Little girls didn't go to the old swimming holes anyway, but they were not supposed to even wade in the creeks during Dog Days. The very time when children could have been enjoying summer cooling, they were afraid of mad dogs and had to stay around the house until Grandma said, "This is the last of Dog Days, and water will not hurt you now."

The dread cry of "mad dog" was apt to strike terror to our hearts any time of the year, but it was especially dreadful in summer. We don't recall any person in our community having been bitten by a mad dog, but there were gruesome tales of dogs with slavering jaws seeking victims, so that the very term "Dog Days" was associated with terror.

Chapter 32

# The Cedar Water Buckets

There are so many improvements in modern homes that it would seem nothing is left for little girls to do. We wouldn't know if the little girls are still required to perform certain tasks around the house as they were back in the so-called good old days. No member of the family except the baby and the toddler was exempt from the regular duties then.

There were the little tasks that little girls and older girls, too, if any older girls in the home, were assigned, and one of the least of these was shining the cedar water bucket—the least task in the eyes of the grownups, but a big job to the little girl who had to muster up the elbow grease for accomplishing the hated task. Not kilowatt power but elbow power was the custom around the turn of the century. Today's little girls, even in modest homes, turn a tap to get water, and they have never seen a cedar water bucket such as stood on a shelf in every home away back when.

There were at least two water buckets on a shelf in the kitchen and another on the side porch. The bucket on the porch shelf held the drinking water, and a bright dipper with shiny black handle hung on a nail near the bucket. The kitchen dipper was a quart-size tin dipper with a short handle for convenience in filling the kettle or for other purposes in cooking.

Every Saturday morning, the water buckets had to be scrubbed and the brass rims made to shine like new gold. Before we were old enough to take on the job, it looked very interesting. "Aunt Mandy" would take the buckets out to the sandy backyard, and then, with a damp cloth dipped in the sand, she would scrub the buckets inside and out until they were sweetly clean and smelling like fresh cedar.

Then, with the cloth and sand, she would start on the brass rims, rubbing vigorously until all the week's tarnish came off on the cloth, and the rims were as shiny as gold dollars. Washed thoroughly and filled with fresh water, the cedar buckets were a joy to see, and somehow the water tasted better than water from our modern spigots.

When we had reached the age to take over the cedar buckets, the job was not so interesting—but hard. With might and main, we scrubbed until aching arms and back rebelled. There was no such thing as slighting the task. Had we dared to skip a spot on one of the buckets, we would be sent back at once to finish the job. When the last rim was bright enough for us to see our faces in and the last bucket back in place on the shelves, we felt proud of our work, but by next Saturday, the whole thing would have to be repeated.

Strange to say, the cedar retained some of its spice aroma as long as a water bucket lasted—if the bucket was cared for, that is. Left too long with no water inside, the bucket would begin to fall apart. It was a sad sight to see a water bucket with rims beginning to loosen and the staves falling apart.

There was poetry in the sight of a shining cedar water bucket and its sparkling contents with the clean dipper at hand. We never dreamed of such things as germs lingering around the family dipper. As soon as a neighbor came to call, we hurried to bring a cedar bucket filled with cold water fresh from the well, and the guest was proffered the dipper.

Grandma didn't believe in such foolishness as "catching any disease by drinking from the dipper."

*Chapter 33*

# Hoecakes on the Hearthstone

Hoecakes baking on the hearthstone of the wide fireplace and the family needing no urging to come and eat—occasionally, on cold winter afternoons, Grandma would have the urge to go back to the ways of her childhood and bake hoecakes in the ashes.

In other regions of our country, the name hoecake does not signify the familiar cornmeal cake baked very thin and brown. We have heard of a few eating places in the North that make a specialty of "jonny" cakes. Not spelled "johnny," this cake no doubt derived its name from the "journey cakes" of frontier days. Pioneers starting on a journey through the wilderness could only take such food as would keep for long periods. Hence, their knapsacks were stocked with cornmeal cakes baked in the ashes of their crude stone fireplaces or even baked in ashes of campfires along the trail.

Many a traveler would have starved had it not been for bits of the sustaining ash cakes that were carefully rationed to last until more food was available.

The slave cooks in the South used to make up the batter for the cornmeal cakes and bake the small cakes on the blade of a cotton hoe thrust in the ashes of their fireplaces. In the big house out-kitchen, the cooks raked hot embers and ashes out on the wide hearthstone and there baked the most tempting hoecakes ever eaten. Hoecakes, these were called—not jonny cakes, which was a Yankee name.

As we remember in the late Nineties, the old out-kitchen of the home built by our great-grandfather was no longer used for cooking purposes as

Illustration of an old iron spider skillet. Circa 1850s.
*Artist Tommy Willis.*

it had been in antebellum days, but in the newer kitchen, there was a wide fireplace, and there were still available the old-fashioned iron utensils used generations earlier.

When Grandma was in the mood, she would scour the iron bake oven, skillet and spider; set one or the other on the hearthstone; and do old-time cooking. Or she might just rake out hot ashes and bake hoecakes such as her own grandmother had baked when America was young.

Water-ground meal, salt and water were the ingredients for hoecakes. Portions of the batter were dropped on the clean hearthstone from which embers and ashes had been raked. Then, when the cakes had become firm, hot ashes were raked over them. Soon, the most tantalizing aroma in the world was filling the kitchen. Grandma knew just when the cakes were brown but not burned. She would rake off the ashes, dust off the cakes with a clean tea towel and hurry them to the table.

We ate them piping hot and slathered with golden butter. The crisp brown crust seemed just made to go with butter, and buttermilk was the natural beverage to accompany this treat. Sorghum or honey was on the table, if we wanted them, but mostly we only used lots of butter with the hoecakes.

Indelibly stamped on our memory are the stories Grandma told us while the hoecakes were baking—how the pioneers came to the South in covered wagons and how they lived on wild game and hoecakes until they were settled into their new log-cabin homes.

*Chapter 34*

# The Straw Bed

Barns all over the South, now bulging with bales of wheat straw since the harvest of the year's grain crop, recall the "straw beds" of Grandma's day. Innerspring mattresses had not been dreamed of. In fact, there were no springs, but plenty of hard slats; and there were the "corded" bedsteads when ropes were crisscrossed to make a springy base for the big straw bed.

Nothing could be cleaner nor more sweet-smelling than the freshly threshed wheat straw piled mountain high in the wake of the thresher. Before the straw was pitchforked into the hayloft, where it was stored for winter roughage for the cattle, there were the straw beds to be made ready.

The women on the place had already washed and ironed their "straw ticks" or bed ticks, comparable to modern mattress-covers but made of heavy cotton ticking. They each had taken down all bedsteads to give them a thorough going over. There being no DDT then, scalding water was used in making bedsteads safe for sleeping. After the bedsteads were back in place in spotless bedrooms (no housekeeper would put a fresh straw bed in a bedroom that had not been thoroughly cleaned), the colored women hurried to fill up bed ticks. If a dry year resulted in shortages of straw, the women were frantic for fear they couldn't fill their beds.

They would hurry to the barnyard with clean striped ticks and fill them up almost to the bursting point. If any were needed for the Big House, in case Grandma was short of mattresses, or as sometimes happened, the family preferred the comfort of a straw bed, the women filled these up first. Then, when every big bed was ready, they were piled high on the wagons. The small children, white and colored, rode triumphantly atop the pile of beds on the wagon, risking a tumble as they rode.

The fresh straw made such a high bed that they almost reached the low ceilings, but what a satisfaction to know that all had clean beds that would last a year. The housewives each tried to outdo her neighbor.

The children often tumbled off the beds in the night before the straw wore down. It didn't take long for the beds to begin to flatten, but they were renewed every morning by a mighty stirring and plumping up of the straw.

The counterpane with the long fringe bought off the peddler hung down to the floor to cover the straw bed, but the odor of fresh straw remained in the house for a long time.

Gradually, the straw wore down until the beds were too flat for style or comfort, and by June, new beds would again be made. The old straw bed was a humble article of furnishing, but it was vastly more sanitary in the home than the cotton mattress that replaced it in later years. The cotton mattress couldn't be renewed and freshened up when it grew lumpy.

Grandma's fine mattresses mostly wore out during the war, and it was a long time after the war before there was money in the Southern homes for replacing such articles. Hence, Grandma had placed straw beds atop the corded four-poster of mahogany or walnut, and atop the straw bed was the big fluffy feather bed.

As a child, we knew the joy of climbing into one of the big beds, which, if made in the country furniture shop, would now be worth its weight in greenbacks. Bits of straw were to be swept from the floor after every making up of the straw bed, but the bed looked neat, and one could sleep high up near the ceiling in comfort. We don't know if any household in modern times boasts such an article as a straw bed.

## Chapter 35

# Lay-By Time on the Farm

The month of August was "lay-by time" in the rural South of horse-and-buggy days. This was the in-between season when farm crops were "laid by," with no more need for cultivation, and the time of harvesting not yet arrived.

These were halcyon days in the South, what with a round of picnics, lawn parties, a big meeting and summer visiting. The horses were rested up and might as well be driven to the buggies, so along the country roads, families or groups of young people were making the rounds of kinfolks and friends. At every home, the premises had been made spic and span. There were watermelons aplenty, vegetables and fruits, yards full of yellow-legged chickens and big hams in the smokehouse, just the right time for having company. And everybody had leisure time—except mother, that is.

If it was election year, there were exciting picnics in the groves with people from all over the county present. If no election year, there were the picnic spots near the river or near a big spring, and young people would drive in their buggies from miles around.

Picnic lunches were no sandwich-and-potato-chips affairs then. The girls themselves helped mother pack big baskets of fried chicken, ham and biscuits, cakes and pies to make the mouth water.

In the afternoons, the neighbors would come, unless you were away from home, and there would be fun around the table in the backyard, eating watermelon or ripe peaches and other fruit.

In lay-by time, little boys frequented the swimming hole and grew as brown as Indians. Little girls, carefully shading their complexions from sunshine, waded in the creek on long summer afternoons that seemed endless.

This was open season for fishing, and men and boys loaded the seines on the back of the buggy, packed biscuits and ham in baskets and drove to the river for seining. About night, they would return, weary but proudly displaying their catches. We would hurry to have a mess of fresh fish for supper.

In lay-by time in the South, spirals of smoke rose lazily from "wash places" all over the countryside. Washerwomen boiled and battled great mounds of clothes for their own families and for their employers' families. Everybody wore cotton and a lot of it.

Lay-by time was hard on light cottons, which had to be repeatedly laundered. But the joy of fresh crisp clothing was worth all the labor. It was pleasant to see the happy washerwomen, their tasks finished, the lines all waving white billows of clothing in the sunshine, and them sitting restfully in their shady yards, smoking their corncob pipes and having fun. None enjoyed lay-by time in the South more than did the good colored people. When their

Imagine washing in a big iron pot and then starching and ironing clothes for these children (from left to right): Cecil, Bill, Clark and Mary Lou Stewart. Circa 1920s. *Authors' family collection.*

farm crops were "laid-by," their houses and yards made immaculate, they had leisure time, and how they enjoyed it.

But all was not rest and fun. There was the ironing to be done—the stacks of white shirts, petticoats, frocks and pillow shams. There was the canning. Every morning a big hamper of fruit would be deposited on the back porch, and mother would organize the work.

Maybe in the midst of paring and cooking, a familiar buggy would be seen coming down the road—a batch of kinfolks arriving to spend the day. Nearly always there was an accommodating "Aunt Mandy" to be called in, and company or no, somehow the canning would be done, the dinner cooked, the ironing done, the yard swept, the vegetables picked and beans strung, the scrubbing done, the cows milked and the butter churned. Mother seldom rested in lay-by time. Time passed on, customs changed, the machine age came to stay and now nobody knows what is meant by "lay-by time." It is only a memory in the rural South.

## Chapter 36

# Sweet Gum Chewing

We noticed in an article recommending varieties of trees to plant in town and country that it was suggested that a sweet gum tree was just right for planting on a city lot. The writer stated that the sweet gum is a stately tree, and its beautiful colors in the fall add to the beauty of a city lot.

Shades of our school days! To think we'd ever find a sweet gum tree in the city. The sweet gum trees grew in the country woods among other trees; and in sun or shade the tree flourished and grew tall. We wonder if there are any of the trees left now in this section and if children know a sweet gum tree from any other tree? If you have one growing in your yard in the city, will you allow boys to "blaze" the tree in order that it may fulfill its purpose? A sweet gum tree is for producing sweet gum, just as an apple tree is for producing apples.

But this generation of youngsters probably has no idea what sweet gum is, and they have never savored its special flavor. Poor underprivileged youngsters, you have never known the fun of working up the crumbling particles that adhered to the blazed section of a sweet gum tree until the particles had become a mass and the sweetest flavored "cud" you ever chewed.

Away back around the turn of the century, children in rural schools knew where every sweet gum tree grew in the vicinity. When boys blazed the trees with sharp axes, a close watch was kept lest somebody steal the gum. After sap had oozed out and dried around the cuts in the tree, it had to be at just the right state before it was ready for chewing material.

With sharp pocketknives, the bits of hard gum were pried off the tree and divided into chewing-size portions. We didn't call in any help; working up the gum was a do-it-yourself project. It was a tricky business, as sometimes gum would stick to the teeth, but if the gum had been gathered at the right stage, it was usually an easy matter to keep chewing until the mass was soft and pliable.

Boys and girls went to school working both jaws with much energy, but when the bells rang for "books," we knew we had to remove the gum and park it beneath the desk top. It was a tragedy when the teacher's eagle eye spotted a gum chewer in school.

"Johnny, come up here and throw that chewing gum in the fire," teacher would call out sternly. And we groaned in sympathy with Johnny—all that good gum gone into the fire.

Mostly the youngsters were adept at the art of avoiding teacher's eye. When called to come to the desk for a recitation, the boy or girl would say to a seat mate, "Here, you want to chew my sweet gum a while?" Sanitation as practiced today was still in the future then. We had no idea that we should not chew another's gum.

Teachers, as well as mothers, groaned inwardly at the thought of sweet gum. How it stuck to little boys' pants, and if a wad was deposited on a little girl's head there was no way of getting it off without cutting out some of the curls.

When chewing gum in fancy wrappers came in fashion, the popularity of sweet gum waned, and before long, no youngster would chew sweet gum. We would love to hear a modern publicity man extol the virtues of sweet gum as a commercial on TV. Wouldn't that be something?

## Chapter 37

# The Quilting Party

S eeing Nellie home" from the quilting party was a pleasure that modern young people have never known. A cold winter night, snow on the ground, the "clop, clop" of a horse's feet, the grind of buggy wheels—or could be just walking the frosty road with Nellie to her home nearby. Lives there a "young" man of the past century who recalls the good old days when pleasures were simple and few but far more thrilling than this generation can realize.

There were two ways of staging a quilting. In the more frequent way, the quilting was an all-day affair. The housewife got her quilt arranged in the quilting frames, planned a company dinner and sent word to her neighbors to come on the appointed day. Some of the women were not skilled quilters, but there were jobs for them to do. One or two would help prepare the dinner, and another might take care of the babies. Mothers with no babysitters at home brought the tots along, and they were deposited in one of the bedrooms, where a volunteer mother looked after them.

Fingers and needles flew, and tongues kept time with both as the quilters sat around the quilting frames. Rural women with no telephones and with neighbors some distance away had fewer opportunities for visiting, and quilting was a good time for catching up with the news.

When the dinner call sounded, all assembled around the long table in the dining room to share such a meal as we seldom see now: baked hen, dressing, rice, gravy, fried chicken, spareribs, sausage, turnip greens, pickled beets, chowchow, sweet potato soufflé, browned Irish potatoes, cornbread, feathery biscuits, fried apple pie, canned damson pie, pound cake and coffee. After an hour of eating and talking, they went back to finish the quilt. Such dainty stitches as they made an heirloom of the quilt, one that the hostess was proud to pass down to her granddaughters.

Long before night, the quilters gathered up their babies and hurried home to cook supper for the men of the house. Happy memories of such quiltings were passed on by Grandma, who lived them over in telling about them to the children.

Another kind of quilting was one held in the evening, and quilters' husbands were invited. When making quilts to be donated to the furnishings of a manse, the affair was held at a spacious home, and couples drove in their buggies, with wives and young girls each bringing their own thimbles and needles. It was a gay scene with the house lighted with kerosene lamps and bright fires roaring up the chimney. Two quilts were put up in two different rooms, and young girls were assigned to one room and the matrons to another. With rivalry concerning who could do the best work and which group would be first to finish, there was much fun. The young men who had escorted their best girls came in for much teasing from the older men, and if it was known that one of the couples planned an early wedding, that young man was teased unmercifully.

Several women helped with the supper, and when all came to the table, there were plenty of oohs and ahs. The sight of that table loaded with every good thing grown on the farms was something to tempt one to eat far too much for comfort. While the kitchen group washed dishes, the quilters completed the two quilts. Then with many goodbyes and last-minute jokes, the crowd hurried off. Girls and boys near enough to walk teamed up with several pairs together for the moonlit walk along the road. Others drove in buggies. "Nothing ever was as much fun as a quilting," Grandma would tell us.

## Chapter 38

# Big Hominy

What a thrill to children of the Nineties when coming home from school nearing sundown to find a fire roaring in the old Iron King and the tantalizing aroma of big hominy cooking floating out from the kitchen. In a day when family meals did not come from the supermarket, but the makings of good nourishing dishes were grown at home with no expenditure save for labor, a simple hot supper was the best meal of the day. And a favorite supper was a dish of "big hominy" with gravy, accompanied by a glass of cold buttermilk.

Big hominy was made of whole grains of corn. Plain hominy—sometimes called grits, but never "hominy grits," as writers from other regions would have us say—was made of ground corn. Corn was ground at the mill for making hominy or grits. It now comes in fancy packages, as there are no old-fashioned mills for grinding the old-time product. While our so-called big hominy was made at home, it also now comes in cans—or at least a facsimile of the genuine big hominy comes in cans.

The real big hominy started with the ash hopper in the backyard. Ashes of hardwood burned in the fireplace were dumped into the ash hopper. Water poured over the ashes leached out the lye. A thin stream of lye trickled from the hopper into a wooden spout that ended in a wooden trough where the lye collected.

Grandma had a supply of lye ready when hominy-making day came around. White corn was shelled and the whole grains dropped into a wooden tub containing water and lye mixed in the proper proportions. The corn was left to soak in water and lye to cover, with frequent stirrings with a long-handled wooden paddle, until the outer husks began to loosen from the grains. Grandma would try rubbing the grains between her hands to see if the husks would come off easily. If not ready, the corn would be left a little longer until a test proved that the husks would shuck off without any bits clinging to the grains.

When all the husks had been discarded and the mass of corn washed, the corn was dropped into a big iron pot with water added and then set on the fire to boil. Grandma kept stirring as the pot boiled, and when she could tell by pinching a grain between thumb and fingers that the corn had reached the right stage, the pot was removed from the fire.

A smaller portion was put on to cook until very tender, with salt, pepper and bacon drippings for seasoning. We could hardly wait for supper, so tempting was the prospect of this delicious food.

We seldom served this plain food for company, but as a family meal, it was equivalent to a feast, along with hot gravy or butter, if we liked.

Any of the hominy to be saved for future use was stored in crocks and kept in a cool place. There was never any to throw away, for we never tired of such a meal.

*Chapter 39*

# Cleaning the Lamp Chimneys

A merican Home Lighting Fixture Month" has been educational—that is, if we took the time to look around and learn what is new in the matter of lighting the home, and then we checked our homes for contrast. When the wizard Edison first began to develop the discovery that eventually led to home lighting, it was enough for the average family to have one fixture in each room, suspended from the ceiling. It was wonderful to be able to snap on a light and see the entire room lighted up after kerosene lamps for so many years.

Grandma and other old-timers thought "no good would ever come of such going against nature." Lamps filled with kerosene, with chimneys bright and shining and wicks trimmed, were good enough for any home. Besides, one could go to the country store and trade in eggs for a gallon of kerosene, which would last for weeks. The new lights cost money, and they were too bright anyway. "Children's eyes will be ruined if they study their lessons by such bright lights," Grandma said firmly.

It was a long time before electric lights came to rural homes, and in the meantime, boys were sent to the store with a gallon tin can, an Irish potato stuck on the spout, for kerosene. Nobody ever bought more than a gallon at one time. On Saturday, the little girls or older sisters made the lamps ready for Sunday. Soapsuds made the glass lamp bowls and chimneys shine like diamonds, but if chimneys were smoked, a little girl's hand was inserted in the chimney to cleanse the grime with a cloth, a job we hated. Burners of brass had to be scoured and made to shine like gold. Wicks had to be trimmed a certain way or else they would smoke when lighted. A sigh of relief was uttered when the row of shining lamps filled with kerosene stood ready on a shelf, representing tedious labor and application of elbow grease. Could be that a careless brother would light a lamp that evening and turn the wick too high. Smoke-blackened chimneys on a newly filled lamp were heartbreaking to a little girl.

We didn't have problems of watts and sockets and short circuits and fixtures; we just had parlor lamps, bedroom lamps, lamps for study tables and plain lamps without any decorations. Many of these are treasured antiques now, but it was a long time after the era of kerosene lamp filling and shining before the one-time little girls began to bring the old-fashioned lamps into their homes and wire them for electric lamps. At the very sight of a kerosene lamp, a groan would go up from the throat of one who had served as lamp trimmer and filler back in other days.

*Chapter 40*

# The Traveling Gin

It's cotton-picking time in the Piedmont, and the highways are crowded with big trucks, filled with the snowy staple, rolling along bound for the cotton-gin. Away back when, the gin came to the cotton, not the cotton to the gin. The annual visit of the traveling gin was a thrilling event to children of the Nineties.

All fall, the cotton crop had been stored in the big cotton-house after being picked and hauled from the fields. The ginning outfit traveled over the countryside from farm to farm, remaining at each farm until the year's supply of cotton had been ginned and baled, ready for market.

Word would be sent out through the neighborhood that the gin was on its way and would be at our place on a certain day. There would be a flurry of making ready for the big job, and extra farmhands were lined up for helping the regular employees of the ginning outfit—the "gin-hands."

Soon we would hear the rumbling of wheels, and into the farm yard the big steam engine would come, escorted by a flock of gin-hands in greasy overalls and big red bandanas. We children, perched on the fence to watch the proceedings, thought "Big Ellick," the engineer, was like something out of Treasure Island. The queer-looking gin would come next and then the wagons with tools and equipment.

With mighty heaving and tugging, the machinery was rolled into place and Big Ellick began to warm up the engine. Its shrill whistling and hissing of letting off steam was almost like a circus, we thought. Then with loud orders and much shouting back and forth, the roar and clickety-clack would resound, and the ginning had begun. Men loaded cotton from the cotton-house into big baskets for "Big Jim," the ginner, to feed into the maw of the gin. Finally, a bale would be turned off, and slowly other bales followed, until the year's crop was ginned.

There were frequent stops to "fix things," and sometimes there were breakdowns so serious that somebody had to go in a buggy to Greenville for new parts for the gin. Then the gin-hands laughed and joked and wasted time until all was in running order again. The boss, or owner, of the outfit had a stock of picturesque language for such occasions as breakdowns and delays, but we children wouldn't leave the scene long enough for him to express his feelings in his own language.

Mother and the colored women had picked chickens, baked chicken pies, made fruit pies, fried ham, baked biscuits and pans of cornbread, steamed big pots of turnips, cabbage and peas and made the usual sweet potato custards to serve with hot coffee, gallons of it, and big pitchers of buttermilk. Nothing came from the store, save sugar and coffee. Two long tables, one for white gin-hands and the boss and one in the kitchen for the colored hands, were loaded with food. The meal was a feast, and there was uproarious fun as they ate, especially at the table in the kitchen.

Now the boss of the ginning outfit sends out trucks to pick up the cotton, and the children never even see the gin.

*Chapter 4*

# The Country Doctor

## Family Physician of the Old School

In the historic Fairview Presbyterian churchyard stands what is believed to be the only monument in the world honoring the memory of the family physicians and the wives of the old-time doctors who kept the home fires burning while the doctor was away on errands of mercy. This monument was erected by Dr. H.B. Stewart, one of the country doctors who now sleeps alongside his colleagues of other days, not far from the monument that pays tribute to the courage and self-sacrificing lives of the old-school family physicians.

In early days, the doctors rode horseback through the days and nights, in all sorts of weather, often up to their horses' knees in mud, undeterred by rain, sleet or snow. Waking up in the wee, small hours of the night, we might hear the "clop, clop" of a horse making its way along the country road, and we would know that the doctor was abroad on an errand of mercy.

Far from a drugstore in that day, the country doctor carried his stock of medicines in his saddlebags. How often we remember the doctor opening his little black bag and saying to one of the family, "Bring me a clean phial." The bottle would be filled with "drops," or the doctor would make up "powders" in twists of paper with instructions of when and how often to take.

The old-school family physician was more than a doctor. He was a family counselor and friend, as well. He knew when John was desperately ill that it was a matter of poor crops and a burden of debt. He knew just what to say to cheer John and start him toward recovery. He knew that a mother's illness was the result of over-work, a big family and no household help, and he knew just what to say.

We have nothing against the modern "specialist," but he can never take the place of the old-time family physician who knew each family's circumstance.

Mrs. Conway Jones and Mrs. Paul Jones, daughters of the late Dr. Andrew Howard, tell of their father staggering from his horse, half frozen at the end of a long ride in extreme weather. "I got down off my horse, put my arms around his neck in order to get warm—otherwise, I would have never been able to get home," the doctor said.

The doctor's wife did her part in helping the doctor to make his rounds: keeping a warm home and plenty of hot food ready when he came in at any hour of the day or night. She often had to render first aid when patients came to the doctor's home badly in need of help. A matter of sponging wounds or binding up a broken arm was all in the day's work for the doctor's wife.

The country doctor was dentist as well. He plunked a patient down on a kitchen chair and without any so-called pain killer, he yanked out the tooth, charging only a quarter. He was obstetrician, pediatrician and setter of broken arms and legs, and with a bottle of blue mass, one of castor oil, another of quinine and the wherewithal for mustard plasters and fly blisters, there was scarcely any ailment that he could not cure.

Heroes all were the family physicians, and their wives were of the stuff of which heroines are made. Soldiers and sailors, statesmen, scientists—all have been immortalized in stone. It was left to Dr. H.B. Stewart to pay tribute to the unsung heroes and heroines who helped to build a nation.

## Chapter 42

# Making Sorghum Syrup

When the frost is on the pumpkin and the corn is in the shock, fall is here. Fall has another significance not relating to corn and pumpkins. Fall is the time for making sorghum in this section of the South. We children could hardly wait for the time when sorghum making would begin.

Sorghum cane grew in patches or big fields everywhere. The canes, cleanly stripped, were piled in the wagon beds to be hauled to the sorghum mill. There was one mill or two in every community, and these did a rushing business in the fall.

Early on a clear morning, we would see smoke spiraling up from the wooded hollow where a mill was located. The odor of fragrant wood smoke together with the sweet odor of the cane made us hurry to get over to the woods and see them make molasses. There was a big rock fireplace, and squarely across and on top of this heating system was a long box lined with metal. The box was divided into compartments for holding juice in the several stages of cooking.

The cane crusher was a clumsy iron affair that would turn around and around by mule power. A patient mule, this being no job for a frisky or fractious mule, would be hitched with chains to the apparatus that crushed the stalks. The stalks were slowly fed into the crusher, where they were ground to a pulp. Buckets or tubs were placed to catch the juice. Sometime a little wooden trough was placed to convey the juice down to the cooking fire. The crushed canes, called "pomace," had to be tossed aside, and soon big piles accumulated. The pomace was considered nothing but a nuisance.

The mule kept going around and around as one big tub after another yielded up its juice. In one compartment of the cooker, the juice was just coming to a boil; in another, the juice was cooking furiously, and somebody had to keep stirring. They skimmed off the foam, which rose to the top of the juice, and children watching nearby could help themselves to the skimmings. Down in the last compartment, the juice was nearing the last stage. It was a beautiful, rich, light brown color, and the fragrance was tantalizing. We would often bring biscuits along with us, and we could nearly always persuade the man who was stirring to lift his paddle and pour hot molasses over our biscuits.

S.L. Coleman was a "Clemson College man" who stirred the syrup at his farm on Fairview Road [Extension]. Circa early 1900. *Authors' family collection.*

Careful watching and stirring was important at every stage of the process, but in the last stage, it was most important. If the molasses scorched from lack of continual stirring, the entire batch of juice was lost. There was an expert at the art of sorghum making in every community. It was incredible to watch him work—stirring, skimming, picking up the paddle and letting a little juice dribble from the paddle. He had no formula for cooking syrup and no time-tested recipe.

"I cook with my eyes," he would say. Experience had taught him when the juice was just right.

"Take her off," he would call out, and men hastened to transfer the perfectly made molasses into big tubs or barrels.

We would carry buckets of sorghum back to the house, where hot biscuits and butter awaited us. A feast, we thought. And other people thought so too, for there was always a market for good sorghum. Breakfast in the fall, with fragrant sorghum syrup along with other homegrown foods, was just out of this world.

## Chapter 43

# Making Lye Soap

Early in the spring when the buds on peach trees began to show color, Grandma and other housewives began to look to the supply of soap-making materials they had saved through the winter. Every meat skin, bone and scrap of fat meat were carefully saved in crocks and kept in the smokehouse until time to make lye soap.

In the backyard was a crude contrivance known as the ash hopper, where deposits of hard wood ashes had been accumulating through the winter. When time approached for making soap, Grandma began to pour water on top of the ashes in the old ash hopper, and the water seeped through the ashes to trickle down in a spout at the bottom of the hopper. The liquid lye poured down from the spout into a little wooden trough, and when the trough was filled, Grandma poured the lye into a big stone jar to keep until needed.

Then when peach buds were just at the right stage and the "signs were right," Aunt Mandy would come early on a sunny morning to help with the soap making. How she loved the smelly job and with what pride she attended the big black pot of boiling lye and grease scraps set on hot coals out in the backyard! The lye would finally eat all the fat off the bones, and then the contents of the black pot would boil up like fury while Aunt Mandy stirred. Taking a chicken feather, the soap-maker would dip it into the pot. When the lye ate the feather down to the stem, the soap was done. Experience was required in addition to the feather test to determine the exact time to pull the hot coals away from the pot and leave the soap to cool. When cool, it would be ladled out with a long-handled gourd and poured into stone crocks. No metal was used in soap making or storing, lest the soap eat holes in the metal.

"Now, ain't it a pretty sight," Aunt Mandy would say as she dipped the gourd into the soap pot, pouring some of the soap back into the pot just to see if it looked right. We children couldn't see any beauty in lye soap; we hated it. Sometimes in a pinch, we had to wash dishes with lye soap in the water if we were out of bar soap, and how the strong soap made our hands raw! The washerwomen liked it because it whitened clothes fully as white as the modern ads claim their "famous" products will whiten all the wash. With hands made raw by the soap, our washerwomen never seemed to mind—such was their pride in having a white wash on the line. They used it for scrubbing floors with the corn shuck–scouring mop, and how the clean floors shone after a lye soap cleansing.

Pioneering housewives had no other kind of soap, as Grandma told us, and how children hated to take baths with such strong soap.

When a fine castile soap became available, a cake would be purchased when a baby was born; and sometimes the cake of fine soap would be carefully saved for the next baby. As a baby grew old enough to stand lye soap baths, the castile soap would be put away. Mothers never knew if any more fine soap would be available when there was need.

Grandma and her grandmother doubtless turn in their graves as their young great-great-great-granddaughters stock cabinets with perfumed soaps, creams, and other luxurious toiletries—a long way from the day of lye soap face washing.

## Chapter 44

# Old-Time Hustings

Strange as it may seem, now that women have the right to vote, very few comparatively attend the gatherings where candidates for offices make their speeches and list their promises of what they will do when elected. Yet back in other days, when women were mere chattels not trusted with the right to vote, women flocked out to the hustings and made a day of it.

All the glamor has departed from matter of what was formerly known as "campaign speakings," or the hustings, now that the old-fashioned picnic has been outmoded. We could hardly wait for the great day to arrive when we should see and hear our candidates and meet our friends at the picnic. For a day or two ahead of the picnic scheduled in our community, there were the candidates making their rounds via the horse and buggy. We were supposed to give them food and lodging; it was a patriotic duty. Some stingy, selfish families would insist, "They expect to make money in office, why should we entertain them for free?" However, it was not so with most families in the country, and not with our family. We had fat fryers in the coop, big country hams in the smokehouse, plenty of apples for pies and big biscuits were always on the menu. On the day before the picnic, we not only prepared the fixings for a picnic dinner, but we also wrung off heads of extra chickens and got all set for a visit from at least one of the candidates.

We remember especially Mr. Plyler, running for school commissioner, and Sheriff Gilreath, who rarely missed spending a night with us before the picnic. These gentlemen came late and left early the next morning, with too much on their minds to allow time for visiting. Soon afterward, we, too, were on our way to the picnic, a huge basket of food under the seat of the surrey and fodder for the horses tied on the back of the vehicle. The road was crowded with buggies, surreys and even wagons as all the neighborhood turned out for the hustings. The picnic site was in a grove of old oaks, and buggies were under the trees all around. Not only our neighbors, but also many people from Greenville were early on the grounds. At dinner, the home folks invited as many outsiders as we could feed, and a good time was had by all. Office seekers were flitting here and there, hardly taking time to eat, shaking hands, smiling, chucking little girls under their chins and maybe kissing babies, but we are not sure about that.

Although the women couldn't vote, they sat in on the speaking and were as interested as the men. After all the work of preparing food, the housewives were still able to sit all day long and then go back home and cook supper for another visiting candidate.

Dinner at the picnic was spread on a big white tablecloth laid on the ground. With so much food, one would think that stooping down for helpings would be hard to do, but somehow, everybody managed to keep stooping,

Fairview descendant John C. Stennis, "Mr. Integrity," Mississippi's U.S. senator (back right), is seen with family in front of the Stennis homeplace (1808) on Peden Road, Fountain Inn. Circa 1960s. *Authors' family collection.*

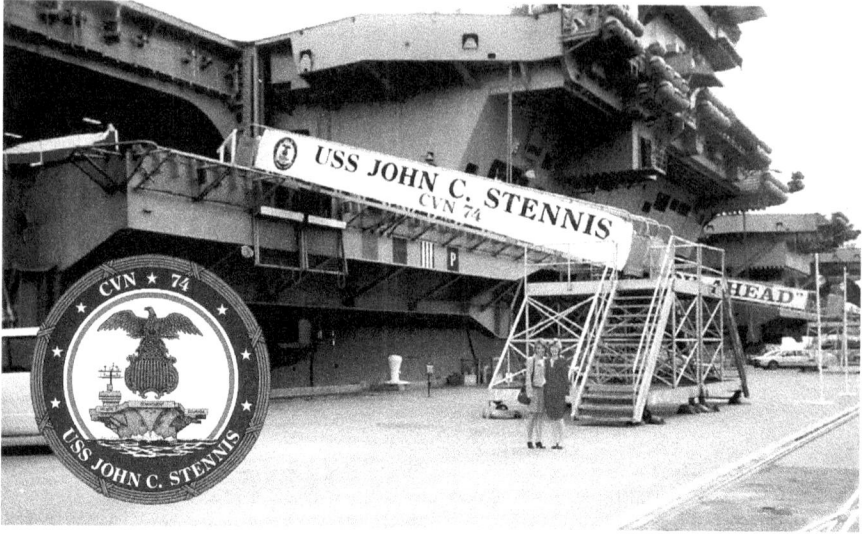

Liz Riner and Mary Huff admire an aircraft carrier commissioned in 1995, honoring their cousin Stennis's service as chairman of Armed Services, Ethics, Standards/Conduct Committees. Circa 1999. *Authors' family collection.*

and seldom was any food left to take home. Then watermelons were cut in various locations on the grounds, and people kept eating at intervals between the speeches.

The speeches were something. There were orators in these days, and even those running for lesser offices had practiced their speeches and could deliver them in thundering tones. It was a favorite theme when speaking out in the country to play up the worth of the dirt farmers against the qualities of the slick city men, especially the lawyers. Farming people were urged to vote "for me—I am a plain dirt farmer, and I'll look out for the farmers' interests. Vote for a lawyer and he will work for the rich man." Sometimes, when after election the candidate failed to make good on his promises to the farmer, it would be remembered, and at the next hustings, the farmers were not slow in taunting him, reminding him that he had failed to make good.

The colorful days of the hustings are gone. Now we can hear speeches on the radio and see our candidates on TV. We no longer expect them to drive up and spend the night, nor do we fry chickens for them to eat at the picnics as in the so-called good old days.

*Chapter 45*

# The Old Rail Fence

Country life in the Nineties offered many joys that modern children have never known. One of these was the fun derived from the old rail fence. The very sight of an old-time rail fence around a field or a mountain home today makes one nostalgic for long days of play along the old fences before barbed wire displaced the "crookedy-crook" of Grandma's day.

The plantation pasture then was a delightful place, with meadowland along the creek bank, woodlands on higher ground and the area separated from nearby fields by the mossy rail fences. If there were any cows with ill dispositions to show unfriendliness toward children who played in the pasture, we confined our playing to the vicinity of the rail fence. At the approach of a cow with lowered head, a sign of a bad mood, we could skip up to the top of the rail fence and down on the other side in double-quick time. No wires were there to catch a frock or a boy's trousers and hold the wearer in a tight grip.

The older the rail fence, the more delights it offered. The fence corners had long been an established home for small wildlife. Young rabbits hopped out from tangled patches of briars, and chipmunks whisked about near convenient dens under big rocks. We sometimes happened on a partridge nest, full of those tantalizing eggs that we yearned to take home, though we had been forbidden to do any such thing. Tiny brown partridges, the most cunning babies of the wild, might come scuttling along in the wake of their beautiful brown-and-tan mother, but we could never catch one. They hurried to blend with the landscape in another fence corner where they became invisible.

There was the thrill of apprehension lest we encounter a black snake, the kind that liked fence corners and baby birds. Bird nests were numerous in the bushes and briars, and birds perched on the topmost fence rails to trill their joy or to utter warning notes at the approach of an enemy. Nests of tiny field mice hidden beneath the lowest rails and grasshoppers in many colors were all about the place.

Fence corners were ideal spots for playhouses, and the wild flowers grew in more variety and abundance in partly shaded fence corners than anywhere else. Daisies, wild roses, goldenrod and nearly every wild flower we had ever heard of grew in some fence corner.

When Grandma sent us to search for the turkey's nest, we were sure of finding it in a fence corner far away from our regular and most frequented spots. The turkey hen liked privacy for her nest, and the seclusion of a rail fence corner ensured her safety

A group of children playing together had fun climbing the old rail fence. "Last one over is a goose egg," one would call out, and with shouts of laughter, we would hurry to win the game. Sometimes our fun was mixed with dread of the sad aftermath. Great three-corned tears in a little girl's skirt or a snag

A stone, not a rail, fence surrounds the Fairview Cemetery. Texan Captain D.D. Peden donated gates to commemorate the one-hundred-year reunion in 1899. *Courtesy of Fairview Presbyterian Church.*

in the seat of a boy's pants meant an interview with Mother, and mothers didn't take lightly such a thing as a snag or torn lace in our clothing.

Then, too, there were often broken rails from our strenuous games of climbing, or we might fail to replace any rails we had carelessly displaced from the top of the fence. Cattle were quick to find such breaks in the fence, and when the cows got out and ate up the corn, there was sure to be a reckoning for the culprits—the human kind, that is.

*Rail Fence Reveries* is the title for a book of poems, mostly singing of country life, a fitting title. Susie Rabb is the author, and her home, Rabbit Hollow, at Cedar Mountain, North Carolina, is partly surrounded by a very old rail fence. The birds and flowers, rabbits and other small animals abound in the vicinity of this rail fence, and the very atmosphere is redolent of poetry.

A neat wire fence is very practical and makes for security, but lovers of the picturesque sigh for the old rail fence.

## Chapter 46

# Sitting Till Bedtime

## Lightwood Knot Fire

A big basket of rich pine knots in the corner beside the fireplace and a pile of the knots and even stumps of pine at the woodpile in the backyard furnished the makings for lighting the home in the rural South after the war. Long after the war, this type of lighting begun in the Sixties by necessity was still used in some of the homes. Economy was still necessary in the waning days of the century, and Southern families had developed habits of thrift that helped them to prosper in the beginning of the twentieth century.

The many pines all over the section were rich in stores that made light. "Lightwood knots" oozing resin were good substitutes for kerosene, and the latter cost hard-earned money. Boys were kept busy through the winter at odd times searching the woods for fallen pines or cutting up logs from the piles of trees awaiting the log-rolling crews. Millions of lightwood knots went up in black smoke unless the boys rescued part of the knots and hauled them to the house, where they were piled up at the woodpile ready for making light.

When fires burned in the big fireplace in the living room on winter evenings, a knot or two from the basket would be cast on the flames. At once, the softest, brightest light imaginable would turn the room into a cozy scene with light for work or play. Grandma and the girls would be busy knitting or piecing quilts, making tatting, spinning thread or mending. There was good light for all these tasks. The menfolk would read the paper or do a bit of shoe repairing by the soft light. The children with their studies or playing games rounded out the family scene. There were no moving pictures then, no radio, no TV. Every night was "family night," unless some of the neighbors came to sit till bedtime or we paid back a visit to a neighbor who had been to our home last.

Sitting until bedtime was a pleasant custom in the rural South. When the dog barked outside, we would rush to the door to see a lighted lantern bobbing along the lane; the neighbors were coming. "Johnny, bring in more lightwood knots," Grandma would say, and another basket of fat lightwood would be brought in.

Tossing lightwood knots on the fire as needed, the family entertained the company. We might parch peanuts and bake apples on the hearthstone, scorching our faces with nearness to the hot flame of the lightwood knot fire, but it was fun to have company and to share our homely refreshments.

Soon after the war, as Grandma told us, there was no other light available save the lightwood knots, and when young girls entertained their beaus in the evenings, they had lightwood knot fires in the parlor. Their mothers saw to it that the supply of lighting material was plentiful.

"See that you don't fail to throw knots on the fire," their mothers would say sternly.

And in later years, the old gentlemen told us that girls were prettier by the light of a lightwood knot fire than when courted by any other light. The lightwood knot flames were so soft that they cast a glow of romance over everything.

One sees, occasionally, bundles of lightwood splinters offered for sale as kindling. These do make good kindling for starting fires, but they are a far cry from the big fat knots that one tossed on top of the fire to burn with sputtering noise and clear golden flames.

*Chapter 47*

# Spring Cleaning in Grandma's Day

Annual spring cleaning has gone the way of other institutions of the good old days.

"Why, I don't do spring cleaning anymore," several housewives have recently told me when I asked about their routine housekeeping. Yet these housewives have attractive homes, orderly and clean. It is just the changing times that have resulted in banishing that dreaded chore of our grandmothers.

When a spell of rainy weather such as we have experienced this spring and early summer occurred away back when, Grandma and her neighbors fumed and fretted over the obstacles to their routine. Spring cleaning had to wait for sunny weather; and when that job was postponed, the entire schedule of tasks was completely thrown out of order. One had to finish spring cleaning before fruit and vegetables were ready for canning and drying, but if weather prevented the cleaning, how could one do the cleaning and the canning at the same time?

If the housewife was late beginning the spring cleaning, that meant rushing to get the job done in time. Grandma would call in extra help, and every worker had to do the work of two in order to hurry up the process. Curtains were quickly taken down and hurried to the wash place, where Aunt Mandy went to work with the washing, and then hurried through the ironing. By that time, several workers had cleaned windows to a sparkling clearness, swept down the walls and hurried the rug up and out to the backyard fence where stout workers did the beating of all rugs to get rid of the winter's accumulation of dust.

Feather beds had to be sunned and the beds made clean and ready for summer. New straw would be put in straw beds after threshing season. Quilts had to be sunned and packed away in chests with tobacco leaves and stems to keep moths away. A mighty scrubbing of pots and pans, cedar water buckets and other household implements had to be done, although such things had been done when needed all during the year. When weary little girls protested that the water buckets and the lamps didn't need more cleaning, Grandma invariably replied, "We must go through the motion of spring cleaning whether it is needed or not." An old-fashioned philosophy, it seems to have been forgotten by this generation.

Modern housewives have push-button gadgets and kilowatt power available, and cleaning is done at frequent intervals. Even windows may be cleaned by workers who can be called in and entrusted to do the job when needed. Rugs are quickly vacuumed on the floors; nobody hangs a rug on a line and attacks it with a beater anymore. Curtains are drip-dried or dry cleaned—no laundering of ruffles these days. There is no such thing as sending little girls to the creek bank for white clay with which fireplaces are made immaculate for summer, and no such thing as whitewashing fences around the yards or sweeping vast areas of sanded yards with brush brooms made of dogwood sprouts.

Better not even mention such a thing, or the garden clubs will come down on you about cutting dogwoods. Modern kitchen equipment is kept gleaming like mirrors with prepared cleansers that work in a jiffy. There is even a frying pan that doesn't require any grease. It's enough to make Grandma whirl in her grave: a frying pan that isn't a crusted black iron affair that yielded up the best fried chicken and country ham the world has ever tasted. But cleaning such a pan—ugh!

Modern housewives have it made. They don't have to go through the motion of annual spring cleaning.

## Chapter 48

# Hilling the Potatoes

Always in other years, the fall was the busiest season in the country. What with cotton-picking, corn-shucking and sowing fall grain, there were dozens of other tasks that must be done in time, or it would be useless to do these jobs at all. One of the fall jobs was taking up the sweet potatoes.

"Time to take up potatoes," Grandma would say when she saw the first light frost appearing on the potato vines.

Just a little frost was needed for the season to be just right, but much frost would ruin the flavor of potatoes. A frost-bitten flavor made the good potatoes unpalatable. So Grandma kept a weather eye out in early fall, lest she miss the most flavorful time for getting the potatoes out of the ground.

Children were eager to have an excuse to stay away from school. Teachers had frequent notes written by parents, saying, "Please excuse Johnny. He had to help take up the potatoes." Naturally, that kind of excuse was valid. Every child on the place, colored children and all, went to the potato patch with pails or baskets early in the morning. One of the colored hands, or two if need be, started cutting off the potato vines, while another man started a big plow down the furrow. As he turned the furrow, out popped the potatoes, and children trotted along picking the potatoes out of the furrow, filling the containers and piling potatoes in designated spots around the field. Others sorted the piles of potatoes, leaving the cut and bruised or the very little ones, called "strings," aside. These would be hauled to the barn for feeding the pigs.

In the meantime, miniature "wigwams" would be going up along the plowed spots. The plowmen had hauled big piles of corn stalks and loads of pine straw from the woods for making "potato hills." They would shovel up a bed of dirt a little higher than the other ground, cover it with a mat of pine straw and then lay potatoes to form a pyramid-like pile. When the pile was high enough, they laid an even cover of dried cornstalks from bottom to top, but in the center they had arranged four pieces of two-by-four heavy planks for a ventilating shaft. Over the cornstalks was a coating of pine needles, and over that, a heavy layer of soil, with either a sheet of heavy tin or some slabs, would be placed over the hill. When all the potatoes were hilled, the field looked like an Indian village of little wigwams.

After several weeks, the housewife would open the side of a hill and bring out a basket of the finest potatoes you ever ate. All through the winter, there would be potatoes keeping in the hill, and they had a flavor and a sweetness different from even the modern potato house product. These days, the farmer hauls his potatoes in crates to the potato house for storage, which is very convenient, and they are dried out to a sweetness that we like, but we miss seeing the wigwams in the potato patches. We miss, too, having to go out on a freezing winter morning to take a basket of potatoes from the hill.

## Chapter 49

# The Days of Log-Rollings

One of the earliest "workings" or cooperative labor projects in the life of early America became the first to be discontinued. The log rolling of pioneer days was a picturesque event. The first of the log rollings was held when the earliest settlers cleared little new grounds and found the labor of disposing of the trees to be more than one man could manage on the do-it-yourself plan. Neighbors found it simple and helpful to combine their efforts, and by the time spring plowing time came around, the logs on each little cleared spot had gone up in smoke. Even as late as the Nineties, there were log rollings in some remote rural areas where virgin forests had been left because the land was not needed.

The woodland owner selected the ground to be converted into a cornfield, then began the operation by "deadening" the huge trees. With sharp axes, the men would go to the woods early in the year before sap rose in the trees and would cut into each tree trunk several feet above the ground, letting the chips fly until a ring had been made around each trunk.

The trees were left to stand until the next winter when the deadening would be complete. It was a pitiful sight—stark withered trees standing where once had been beautiful forests. We remember how the great trees looked with limbs bare and the ground littered with dead twigs.

When time came for a log rolling, the neighboring farmers would be invited, and they would come with their axes. Soon, all were at work, and the forest rang with the sound of axes. Dead trees were cut down, big limbs chopped off and the trunks cut into lengths that could be handled for rolling.

Then while some chopped, others were rolling the logs into huge piles. Only men of brawn could handle big logs, and it seems incredible now that neighbors would willingly help with such hard work. But the same group went from one neighbor's field to another's until all new grounds in the neighborhood had been cleared of logs. The piles of brush were left at the side of the cleared spot, and the piles of logs were burned where they had been rolled.

It was a sight we shall never see again, and it was not a common sight in the Nineties. We remember witnessing two log rollings, and Grandma told us that these cooperatives had been a familiar part of life in the South in her younger days. When fires had been started in the log piles, somebody had to watch them carefully. One man was set to tending the fires while others went on with the log rolling.

During the day, big pots of hot coffee were kept on the ashes where the men worked, and they drank coffee in big tin cups. At the same time, they would eat sweet potatoes roasted in the ashes. Only by replenishing their strength in this way were they able to keep on with such strenuous labor.

At noon, they were summoned to dinner by the welcome sound of the blowing of the conch shell. As they trooped into the house, they were greeted with the cheerful sight of long tables covered with home-woven tablecloths and loaded with food fit for working men. The housewife and colored helpers would also be assisted by some of the neighbors, who has worked through the morning to prepare a huge feast of big pots of chicken with dumplings and platters of beef (the farmer nearly always killed a beef for this occasion). There would be ham with red gravy, bowls of black-eyed peas, turnip greens, pans of cornbread with cracklings all through them, big biscuits and sweet potato pie or pudding. Pitchers of buttermilk and great pots of coffee completed the meal.

The last log would be consumed in flames before it was time for the workers to leave for home, but a man on the place was always required to sit through the night to watch, lest dying embers suddenly revive and a dangerous fire get started.

When logs began to be worth money, the practice of log rollings and burnings ceased.

## Chapter 50

# Old Country Schools
# and Half-Moon Pies

I t's back to school for youngsters all over the South when September comes. Going to school in modern times in modern buildings with all that goes to make school attractive is vastly different from going to school in the Nineties.

When the old hand bell rang out for "books" in the country school in the late Nineties, children of various ages, from tots to late teens, crowded into the little one-room schoolhouse. Only in rare cases were these school buildings with more than one room until after the turn of the century. Ours was not the "little red schoolhouse" of song and story. The rural schoolhouse in the South was a little frame building, its unpainted sides weathered to a soft gray. There was one door to the schoolroom and several small paned windows.

Fieldstones were used in building the chimney at the end of the room and in constructing a wide fireplace, which never seemed to warm the room.

The timbers had shrunk, and fresh winter winds crept through the cracks. Pupils walking miles to school over frozen roads were almost numb with cold when they reached the schoolhouse. Teacher and the bigger boys had a fire roaring up the chimney. The children had to come in relays to stand before the blaze, and while one group thawed out, those away from the fire shivered with cold. Wood was cut and hauled by the patrons, and the bigger boys took turns with the axe, cutting the piles of logs in the schoolyard into fireplace lengths.

A shelf outside the door held the cedar water bucket with its long-handled dipper. The communal dipper was used, as the word "germ" was unknown in that day. "May I get a drink," or "May John and I go to the spring?" were requests continually heard by teacher—anything just to get out of the schoolroom for a few minutes.

There were no grades, just classes, and while a second reader class was reciting, lined up before the teacher's desk, others were supposed to be studying their lessons. But a pupil who was the picture of meekness might be plotting mischief. Teacher learned to recognize the signs. "Johnny, bring that sweet gum to the desk," or "Mary, put down that book you are reading and study your lessons," teacher would call out as her reading class droned away.

There were no blackboards as we first remember, and when blackboards were finally installed, we thought we were really being "modern." Slates were in vogue, and what a screeching of slate pencils, with annoying requests: "May I wash my slate?" Slates were washed out at the water bucket, with water poured on with the dipper. Some of the boys, sneaking a look at teacher, "cleansed" their slates by spitting on them—no germs then.

Former one-room schoolhouse teachers sisters Cinnie and Carrie Sprouse, in their eighties, sit and talk on Cinnie's front porch. Circa 1960s. *Authors' family collection.*

A welcome sound—"dinner recess"—and we had a long time for dinner and fun. We gathered in groups to sit on the woodpile or rocks in the schoolyard. The oldest girl in each family was in charge of the family dinner basket. The contents included big, feathery biscuits with ham or sausage between the halves; baked sweet potatoes; "stickies," or squares of gingerbread; and, invariably, "Half-Moon" pies, made of dried fruit spread on half a circle of biscuit dough, with the other half folded over and the "half-moons" fried in an iron skillet. Some families brought molasses in wide-mouthed bottles and filled biscuits with the syrup. That was a day when the word "vitamin" was still in the future. Hot dishes were not thought necessary then. We ate our sausage and ham, pies and gingerbread, and thought how much more fortunate we were than Abraham Lincoln and Andrew Jackson, who probably had to settle for a hunk of cold corn bread and a gourd of water from the spring.

We do not remember grumbling about our lack of advantages, and somehow our boys and girls from one-room country schools held their own with others from larger schools when they went to college. And we wonder now how the great of the land who came from country schools ever achieved greatness without being sent to school in modern "palaces" such as our children now have all over the land.

## Chapter 51

# The Day the Preacher Came

The preacher was a man apart from all other men back in the long ago days, and when the preacher came to visit, it was tragic if we had nothing in the pantry for a good meal—if it was a spend-the-day visit, that is. It was not customary then to invite company to come on a stated day—that wasn't done. Not even did Grandma tell the preacher to come next Wednesday and stay for dinner. She wholeheartedly and with traditional Southern hospitality invited her friends, including the preacher and his wife, "to come and spend the day with us any time."

Neighbors coming to spend the day would arrive by half-past eight in the morning, and the female visitors would tie on big aprons and all get to the kitchen to prepare dinner, talking and having a good time as they worked. But it was not the same when the visitors were the preacher and his wife. The familiar buggy was seen coming down the road something like ten o'clock in the morning, and when we saw it coming, one of the children would be sent tearing around to summon one of our faithful colored women on the place. Even that late in the morning, a frying chicken would have to be caught, dressed and plopped into the frying pan. Unless it happened the preacher was known to be particularly fond of country ham, and we could get by just with serving a big platter of ham and a bowl of red gravy.

Every family had ham, and it was not considered a "company dish," but if there was not time to dress chickens, we sometimes had to make do with ham. Aunt Mandy could knock up a batch of fluffy biscuits in short time, and if no fruit for pies, she made egg custards, the best of all desserts. With coffee and rice or potatoes, this was not such a scanty meal.

The dignified preacher tied his horse to the hitching post and, with solemn mien, approached the front door. By that time, Grandma was composed and on her own dignity, wearing a white company apron that she had hastily tied on over her house frock. Greeting the visitor cordially, she would insist that he let one of the boys put up his horse and run back to the kitchen and get busy—he would stay for dinner. We children were glad when the preacher's wife accompanied him, for somehow wives of preachers were more "like folks" than were their husbands in that day. We couldn't understand why Grandma, if she wasn't expecting the preacher for dinner, was more put out when the wife was along. "Men don't notice things as women do," Grandma would say, but we couldn't understand it.

While the dinner was prepared—and we ate early dinner—one of the family members tried to talk to the visitors or showed them the family album. We were glad when we were summoned to the dining room, though

*Left*: The 1700s Scottish collegiate ancestor "Peden the Prophet" inspired many Fairview sons. Reverend William Warren Sprouse, Presbyterian College, Hampton Sydney, Union Theological Seminary. *Authors' family collection*.

*Right*: Will refused to let a wooden leg hinder his education, his marriage to Lila Bear and his founding of the Staunton, Virginia Third Presbyterian Church. Pictured circa 1920, with mother Mattie. *Authors' family collection*.

one little girl had to swish the fly brush over the table if it was summertime. Somehow, the preacher always enjoyed eating, and he didn't seem so solemn as he ate and talked.

After the meal, when all of us went back to the living room, the preacher would seize the opportunity to ask the children questions in the Bible or Catechism. We were frightened until we were almost dumb, and with crimson faces, we managed to stammer out answers that would have been easy in other circumstances. Some of the ministers understood how embarrassed the children were and excused their seeming ignorance, while others were so stern they never seemed to have been children themselves. As we remember, the preacher seldom laughed or told jokes. He was a zealous guardian of his solemn dignity.

There was a tradition that our old church had one time called a pastor who was fat and jolly. The stern brethren had rebuked him for his lack of solemnity, and he had replied, "A Christian has a right to be happy," a statement almost amounting to heresy in that day.

However, we respected our preacher and looked on him with awe. As soon as his buggy rumbled out of our yard, we children evaded Grandma's vigilance and rushed off from the house to shout in freedom.

## Chapter 52

# Winter Wedding and Infare

Winter weddings were in fashion when Grandma was a girl, for somehow brides seemed to prefer Christmas or January for a wedding date. Things were comparatively at a standstill on the farm in midwinter, the family had more leisure to prepare for a wedding and the hosts of kinfolks could take time off to come to the wedding.

The entire fall was a busy time in the house when a wedding was scheduled, as mothers and daughters sewed and quilted and hemmed sheets, getting the bride's chests of linens, quilts and blankets ready for her new home. No self-respecting bride would start housekeeping without stores of bedding and linens. Such things had to be made at home; they could not be purchased ready-made, as in this era.

Even the well-to-do planters in the South were careful of expenditures, at least those whose veins ran with Scotch-Irish blood. The planter might give his daughter a servant girl to accompany her to her new home, and the household furnishings, feather beds, pillows and such were furnished by the bride's parents, who had long been saving against the day when a daughter would marry. The groom or his parents furnished the farm and home where the young man would take his bride. And if a girl was so foolish as to marry a man without a home to take her to, it was said of her that "she is driving her ducks to a poor market."

When the crowds of friends and kinfolks gathered to celebrate a winter wedding, they were invited to stay for the wedding supper, a feast that excelled all other feasts. The bride's family opened up the smokehouse and

A parlor wedding in 1907: Anderson Stewart and Cinnie Sprouse. *Authors' family collection.*

brought out whole hams to bake for the supper. A calf would have been killed, while chickens and ducks by the dozen were dressed for the supper. Great tubs of boiled custard or syllabub accompanied the scores of cakes, and by the time the feast ended, we wonder how the young people could dance through half the night. But a wedding did not come every night, and so the festivities went on.

But by the next morning, a merry group was ready to set off on horseback for the infare at the home of the groom's parents. The bride, arrayed in her second-day dress, might ride in a high buggy with the groom driving, but the party of young people rode horseback, as Grandma said. Along the way, the boys slashed at the jack frost with their riding whips and teased the girls unmercifully. Some of the boys had brought colored bottles along in pockets of overcoats, and as they rode, they tossed the bottles against rocks by the roadside. The sun shining on the broken glass particles turned the roadside into such colorful prisms like no other sight in the world, Grandma said. The bottle shattering was for noise as well as color, and long before they reached the scene of the infare, their approach was heralded by tinkling glass and merry shouts and songs.

The bridegroom's parents had been busy getting ready to welcome the new daughter, and the groom's mother, determined to sustain a reputation equal to that of the bride's mother, was on her toes seeing that everything went off just right. Servants were bobbing and smiling, with male servants taking charge of the horses, and women servants taking wraps, ushering in the guests and helping with the feast, all in honor of "young massa's new bride."

The infare feast was equally as elaborate as the wedding feast, and there was even more fun, for the newly marrieds were subject to continual teasing, and a new stock of jokes had been thought up just for the occasion. Grandma said that she as a young girl would be able to eat hardly anything for a week following a wedding and infare, with such feasting and so much food that it sickened one to think of it afterward. The bride and groom could eat very little with so much teasing going on. All agreed that a winter wedding was preferable to a wedding in spring and summer, as there was time for fun and dancing.

*Chapter 53*

# Grandma's Cures for Colds and Quinsy

Pokes of dried horehound leaves, bunches of green pine tops, dishes of honey, bunches of onions and the kerosene and turpentine handy with cakes of tallow at hand. No, not a magician's supplies—just stuff for curing a cold away back when. This is the season when that great plague of the human race, the common cold, is running rife.

"There is no cure for a cold," modern doctors tell us. Even science, which has come up with discoveries for alleviating such scourges as typhoid fever, diphtheria, smallpox, even polio and tuberculosis, to an extent, dares to say there is no cure for a cold.

We were born in the wrong century. Back in the Nineties, Grandma did not know there was no cure for a cold. She rolled up her sleeves and went into battle when coughs and sneezes heralded the onslaught of a cold or sore throat or quinsy or pleurisy. And she had *Dr. Chase's Recipes* in a big thick volume, published even before her time, to back her up in her own formulas for curing a cold. The sad fact that the "cures" were worse than the colds is still fresh in the memory of everyone who lived through such times.

There was first the dose of castor oil—not the refined, flavored drugstore product but a yellowed sticky mess in a big quart bottle in the pantry. Into a big iron cooking spoon went the oil to be covered with thick homemade blackberry wine to "take the taste out." It didn't. There was no use for a child to plead or to cry—children didn't refuse to take medicine in that era. You opened your mouth, swallowed down the nauseating mess, gagging and inwardly rebelling, promising yourself, "I'll never make my child take castor oil."

Next came the various "teas." There was a tea made from green pine needles—awful. There was another tea made of horehound—also awful. Don't forget the tea made of senna leaves—terrible. Dr. Chase recommended a tea with lemon, hot lemonade, but Grandma differed from Dr. Chase. Lemonade was too pleasant to take for a cold. Then there were the poultices. A red flannel cut like a little jacket, greased all over with tallow and then rubbed with kerosene and turpentine was put on the youngster's chest and rib cage. If there was much coughing, the child was dosed with honey and vinegar. Then dosed and poulticed, the youngster was put to bed to "sweat it out." Next day, if he was still living, he was up and going through more of the treatments.

Dr. Chase advised that no one omit taking a weekly bath as a help to prevent colds.

Onions were invaluable in curing colds, according to Chase's recipes. George Washington was said to cure himself of a cold by eating a hot roasted onion just before stepping into bed at night. To hasten this cure, Dr. Chase said it would help to eat hot roasted onions several times during the day. We could never prevail on Grandma to substitute onions for castor oil.

If a sore throat or quinsy accompanied the cold, an infallible remedy was a red flannel cloth or an old woolen sock rubbed with lard and a mixture of vinegar, turpentine and kerosene and then bound around the throat. One can imagine the fragrance of the premises from all this mixture of cold cures.

## Chapter 54

# Bliss of Shedding Copper-Toed Shoes

Blessings on thee, little man, barefoot boy with cheeks of tan." The poet's theme didn't even begin to describe the bliss experienced by a youngster when the time came to "go barefooted." Almost equal to Christmas was that anticipated day when mothers gave permission to shed the shoes and stockings.

A long, cold winter, with heavy copper-toed shoes for boys and stout shoes for girls on school days—Sunday buttoned shoes could not be worn to school—and how weary the youngsters were of such footwear as spring came on! Heavy black cotton stockings, fastened securely above the knees to "Ferris waists," left freedom for exercise, but the bulk of such hosiery seemed almost unbearable in April.

The majority of families held to the old rule: keep on the shoes until the first of May. Dire predictions of illness sure to result from going barefoot before May first were heard from old-timers.

You were sure to catch colds or come down with the quinsy or pneumonia. Even consumption had been known to result from youngsters shedding their shoes too early.

That dreaded word "consumption" was enough to make children grow pale with fear. We had heard the disease discussed in such harrowing description that we didn't dare shed the shoes in secret—hardly ever, at least. If on a picnic April Fool's Day, when we had run away from school after shutting the teacher out, we celebrated by wading in the creek, we were conscience stricken for weeks afterward.

Certain families were less strict than others and their children more daring. No punishment awaited them if they pulled off shoes and waded in the creek before the orthodox date for such things. It was just painful to those of us who were required to obey the rules or else to have to watch others step forth in freedom on April first, while we had to wait longer.

There was always somebody to tell on us if we dared disobey just once. Even when we managed to elude being found out, our fear of consumption haunted us for weeks. Every time we had a cold or even sneezed, we knew that our sins had found us out. We had gone wading in the creek against the rules, and consumption would catch up with us.

Finally came the day when it was barefoot time, and the bliss of throwing the old shoes in the closet was unspeakable. The feel of cool grass and sand to the bare feet was delicious. Then came the stone bruises and stumped toes, the bite of the rocky ground that almost crippled children that time of the year. But after a few days, running and leaping was easier on the toughened soles.

Even the girls went without shoes and stockings all summer, save for Sunday and dress-up occasions, which were few. Some foolish mothers forced their little girls to wear shoes in summer "to keep their feet from growing too large." It was a disgrace for a young lady to have large feet, and as feet grew rapidly in summer when unrestricted by shoes, it was believed that a girl would have dainty feet when she grew up if she had never gone without shoes. Such mothers, however, were few, and other children pitied poor little girls in shoes while their playmates were free.

We never thought the day would come when young women took no thought of the size of their feet and even grown women would go about without shoes in summertime, feeling no embarrassment but rather proud of their adherence to "style."

## Chapter 55

# Early American Dye Pot

No article of furnishing was more important in early American homes than the dye pot. Glowing red, cool green, soft wine and russet, with all shades between came out of the dye pot to brighten the clothing and accessories of long ago, and the materials for making dye grew in the woods and fields about the homes.

In the Sixties, Southern women revived the art of dyeing, which had been passed down through generations of their families. Even in the Nineties, old-fashioned housewives were still making occasional use of the dye pot, because they liked to make up colors, and there was the thrill of seeing a drab article emerge from the boiling pot in a new bright color that would last. Store dyes were not dependable, but the old tried-and-true herb dyes retained their color as long as a bit of the material lasted. Each housewife had her own "secret" formula for making dyes, and there was friendly rivalry among neighbors concerning excellence of results from a favorite formula.

Mrs. Alberta D. Edwards of Fountain Inn remembers going with her grandmother, the late Mrs. William DePriest of Rutherford County, North Carolina, to search for various herbs and barks to use in making dyes.

The wild yellow daisies that grew along the edges of the fields made beautiful, clear, yellow dye. For a red dye, the bark from wild cherry trees made a glowing red that never faded. A soft wine color was obtained from ripe pokeberries, and a rich green was made from green walnut hulls. When green, the black walnut hulls made green dye and, when ripe, made a dark shade of brown. The grandmother made a rust-colored dye by boiling plain red mud in water until the desired shade was attained.

The big iron pot in the backyard would be filled with water, the herbs or bark tossed into the pot and a fire kindled. Continual stirring with a stout stick or paddle was necessary. When her experienced eye told her that the dye was ready, she strained the contents of the pot. What was left after immediate use was stored in stone churns or crocks for later use. The backyard was a colorful sight on dyeing day, with banners of bright colors waving in the breeze.

Evidently, Grandmother DePriest inherited dyeing secrets from her own grandmother, as beautiful quilts passed down to Mrs. Edwards, some of them made by her great-great-grandmother, are made of tiny pieces of material, some of which were dyed in the soft shades produced by herb dyes, the colors still exquisite. A Rocky Mountain quilt with a bunches-of-grapes design is a priceless antique for the tiny stitches and blending colors.

In our own community, we recall the woolen material made from wool grown on the farm-raised sheep. Walnut hulls with copperas dyed the woolen jeans to a rich brown. Boys from families where wool was produced wore winter suits dyed brown, and the color was fadeless. We children in the Nineties went to school wearing home-knit stockings or socks, dyed brown, and we hated them. Yet they lasted without ripping or snagging. When home-knits were outmoded in favor of heavy, black-ribbed cotton stockings from the store, we turned up our noses at the old-fashioned youngsters who had to wear the home-knit numbers.

Grandma told us that in the Sixties, when there was mourning in every home, there were pots of black dye boiling all over the South. It was unthinkable to wear colors when in mourning. Southern women even wore underwear and handkerchiefs dyed black.

The somber black never grew rusty or pale, and black garments were worn long after the family was no longer in mourning. Our people were too thrifty to discard a frock as long as it was good for more wear.

Now if we dye anything, we run down to the store for packaged dyes. It is much less trouble, and nobody wears out a garment anyway. It "goes out of style" before being worn out.

# Chapter 56
## The Old-Time Hats

A week to stimulate interest in new spring hats? Whatever is the need of anything to stimulate a woman's interest in a new spring hat—save the hat itself or the sight of a lot of hats in the shop windows? Recently, we have noted flowers blooming in shop windows, window gardens of hats as it were, and feminine noses are pressed to the glass windows as girls of all ages revel in the sight of the hats.

Spring hats are always lovely, but this year, they are more than ever tempting and beautiful. Nearly every hat is covered with flowers, and pray—where are flowers more in the right place than on a girl's spring bonnet? Gay flowers, ribbons and luscious colors go to make the hat or bonnet that you will be wearing before Easter this year.

Who wants to wait until late in April to come out in spring array? A girl wants to select her hat early in these modern times and announce her appearance as a frontrunner of Easter. She just can't wait! How can she go through the best part of spring wearing last year's hat, while Easter delays appearing until it is almost May?

Away back when, it was customary to have the new hat on the first of May—not any earlier. As the flannels were not shed until May 1, it was not officially spring until then. On mild April days, it seemed hard to have to wear old velvet hats to church, but even if we had spring hats, we saved them until May. Annually, toward the latter part of April or early in May, rural women and their daughters would drive to Greenville for a day's shopping. Not the least item on the list was the spring hat or hats for little girls and mother.

Young people in church hats in the Fairview Sunday school class. Circa 1900. *Authors' family collection.*

Arriving in the city and leaving the horse and buggy in a hitching lot on Main Street, we set off to see the wonders of the stores. The millinery displays in the Mrs. McKay's shops or Miss Rogers's and others were mouthwatering to the little girls. Wide leghorns; drooping brims wreathed with daisies, forget-me-nots or roses; and with streamers of pink or blue ribbon—these were hats for little girls. For older girls or young ladies, there were gorgeous creations of chiffon or horsehair braid trimmed with roses, lilacs, violets and ribbons. Milliners bought pattern hats, and these were copied by apprentices who sat in the back room and worked all day creating dainty hats. Miss Ida Austin, one of the old-time milliners, said there were no "hours" for work. They worked early and late for a sum that wouldn't buy a girl's lunches now.

Expert salesladies tried on the hats and cooed over us until we just had to have the certain hat, and never have we been any happier than when that lovely creation was packed in a box for us to take home.

There were a few more conservative hats for older women. A woman of thirty years, then, wore plain hats in sober colors, but even the hats of this type were trimmed with discreet bunches of daisies or lavender flowers. The "ready-to-wear" hat came in fashion around the turn of the century. Then every woman had to have two new hats, one "dress hat" loaded with trimming for wearing to church and a ready-to-wear hat with only a band of ribbon around the crown for wearing to picnics or shopping trips. Only ready-to-wear hats were worn with coat suits or tailored frocks. Now the girls step out in tailored suits topped with a hat like a basket of flowers, but we love the flowered hat and the plain suit. A "week" to spur our interest in spring millinery? Just the sight of a new spring hat on any head or in any window and we know that spring is here with hats and flowers and ribbons and veils.

## Chapter 57

# The House amid the Honeysuckle Vines

Nostalgic memories recalled whenever a group of the girls of away back when get together always call to mind the utter lack of modern conveniences in the homes of the good old days. How we were happy and enjoyed life then, despite many of the essentials now a part of our way of life.

There were no kitchen sinks, no bathtubs except those of the tin tub variety and the bowl and pitcher in every bedroom represented luxurious living. In the great houses as well as in more modest dwellings, there was the same lack of such conveniences, yet nobody knew any other way of life, and we didn't miss what we had never had.

There was the well-remembered retreat in a bower of honeysuckle vines or climbing roses at the end of a flower-bordered garden path in the farthest corner of the garden. Housewives in the more pretentious homes used their ingenuity to beautify this garden path. Beds of thyme and tansy, clumps of lavender, scattered daffodils and johnny-jump-ups grew beside the path. Tall hollyhocks nodded their stately heads above the path, which was kept clean of weeds and trash. Sometimes grapevines on fences bordered the path, and the honeysuckle and roses had to be cut back occasionally, lest they overrun the entire corner of the garden.

Southern ladies in hoop-skirted gowns strolled along the garden path, stopping to pick posies along the way. After the noon meal was finished, little girls could be seen hastening along the path toward the only retreat where they might safely remain until somebody else washed the dishes. Many times, they might remain hidden for as long as they dared, only to find the dishes still unwashed and their task awaiting their return.

And in a day when the Scotch-Irish frowned on any book known as a novel as a work of Satan, older girls in the family managed to retreat to the bower beneath the honeysuckle vines and get in some reading of the forbidden novel. The book could be secreted in a hiding place among the thickest of the vines, and how hard it was to have to quit reading lest one attract suspicion by staying away from the house too long.

"Smart boys" thought it great fun to hide out and scale a shower of pebbles in the direction of the honeysuckles, when their sisters had girlfriends visiting them. An inevitable session with the peach tree switch resulted when their sisters told on the boys.

One mother we knew had so many children that she couldn't even find an opportunity to read her Bible, with continuous calls of "Mother." She solved her problem by keeping her cherished little testament in a corner beneath the eaves of the retreat behind the vines. Thus she could spend a quiet period of reading her Scriptures, several chapters a day, in the one spot where an unwritten "Do Not Disturb" was respected.

We believe that the restoration of the Governor's Palace at Williamsburg includes two covered paths screened by evergreen vines, leading to two of the familiar garden retreats in the back garden. At the old Mansion Oakley Park in Edgefield, restored by the United Daughters of the Confederacy restoration, included a similar bower of vines and shrubs. Except for such rare instances, the modern generation would never get a complete picture of the Southern way of life in other years.

*Chapter 58*

# Day of the Cure-alls

Not long after New Year's Day in the Nineties, the patent medicine vendors began to take in the cash. Somehow, there was invariably a rash of aches and pains after the "big dinners" every day for a week. And the sudden change to hog jowl and collard, turnip greens and buttermilk with crackling corn bread didn't cure the mysterious ailments. The doctor was several buggy miles away, and he charged one dollar per house visit. Unless he was tactful and sympathetic with a patient who complained with much groaning and growling about the "awful suffering" of rheumatism or neuralgia, the doctor couldn't manage a cure, and it took a long time to get results—unless the patient resorted to "patent medicines" with their sure cures.

No matter how much the weary family physician might want to say, "There is nothing the matter with you except too much of the wrong kind of food and too much feeling sorry for yourself," he had to look sorry for the poor sufferer. He had to measure out "drops" and make up little "powders" in tiny pieces of paper from the contents of large bottles in his satchel and leave these with directions. If the powders and drops were harmless sugar and water, the patient didn't know it.

Sometimes the aches and pains wore off, but otherwise, the sufferer just sent to the general store for a bottle of that cure-all advertised on posters tacked to the outside wall of the store building. It wasn't long until the sufferer had perked up after having faithfully consumed one or more bottles of the stuff that tasted awful.

If the cure-alls were half iron and half cheap whisky, as we were told much later, nobody knew it then, and the fact that the patient felt strong and perky after such dosage was a surefire testimony to the strength of the "cure."

On the outer walls of every general country store, gaudy ads for the then-familiar patent medicines flaunted their wares. In every newspaper of the day were the patent medicine ads, mostly on the front pages of all newspapers. An engraved hand pointed to the ad, and there were little figures calling attention to the paragraphs, which extolled the cure-alls—belles with bustles, cherubs, doctors with long beards, flags, young mothers holding up smiling babies—all demanding your attention.

There were the heart-rending stories along with the ads, how this mother was so low with weakness and pains in the back that her poor little children were neglected, but then she just began taking certain nerve tonic, and in no time, she was as fine and fit as a fiddle. There was the man who, in the last stages of consumption, switched to a sure cure for consumption, and it worked. Of course it did, for you see his picture along with the ad, and he is in blooming health.

Now there is glowing hope in the year just dawning. Throw away the old pokeberry root and whiskey that your grandmothers used and all that old blue mass and calomel—out of date stuff—and take this wonderful new cure to "start the New Year right." And so the Gay Nineties sufferers filled the cash boxes of the patent medicine makers, and the ads flourished in all the newspapers and periodicals. It was a gay time when rheumatism was banished and consumption could be cured.

*Chapter 59*

# Christmas in the Sixties

The story of Christmas in the South in the Sixties should be recalled each year as we celebrate Christmas in our abundance. Grandma considered it her duty to gather her grandchildren around her on a winter evening when all was in readiness for our Christmas festivities and tell again the story of faith and courage and sacrifice in Southern homes in the day of the Sixties. It was a strange and touching story to us but infinitely strange to modern children who know little about the meaning of sacrifice.

In the Old South, Christmas was celebrated in almost an Old World manner with customs and festivities shared by everybody on the plantation. At the "Big House," there would be lavish entertainment and giving of gifts. Every servant on the place received "handouts," and there was feasting and dancing in the quarters. In 1860, as the dream world of the South faced a crisis, the Negroes still sang happily in the fields. Romance and glamor still held sway. Southern belles and beaus danced the Virginia reel, cotton still whitened on the plantations of Dixie and Christmas we celebrated in the old joyous way—for the last time.

Before Christmas 1861, Fort Sumter had been written into history. One by one, the gallant men in gray had ridden off to join the fight that "would be over before breakfast." Older and wiser heads were serious as the young men were eager to get into the fray, yet old and young were both loyal to the Southland, and now the casualty lists were growing longer. The shadow of hardship loomed over the South, but on the plantations, there was an abundance of homegrown foods for the Christmas feast.

*Left*: CSA captain Samuel McKittrick was married by his brother John, a Fairview minister. He was killed in the Battle of Atlanta on July 23, 1864, at age forty-five. His body was returned in a neighbor's wagon for a Fairview burial. *Authors' family collection.*

*Right*: Samuel's widow, Mary Ann Stennis McKittrick, about forty, is seen in Confederate mourning dress/widow's weeds. After the war, she returned with five young children to the Stennis homeplace. *Authors' family collection.*

The blockage was being enforced and supplies were dwindling, yet gifts were still obtainable. Silks for the ladies, toys for the children, tea and sugar were hard to obtain, but soon the blockade would be lifted and the ports wide open.

Grandma and her friends asked the cooperation of their children in waiting for better times when gifts would be available for everybody. Handouts for the servants were less generous, but the loyal colored people were self-sacrificing. They, too, had faith that the war would soon be over and happy days would come again to all on the plantation.

In 1862, only the children had a right to Christmas gifts, and those were mostly last year's dolls with new dresses and last year's toys mended. Christmas dinner was less abundant, as even homegrown foods were not so abundant. Families willingly grew food for men in the army and lived on less at home. With their father away at the front, Grandma's boys and girls could understand the need for sharing food with the soldiers.

In 1863, Christmas was bitterly cold. Anxious wives and mothers had troubled thoughts of loved ones, poorly clad and fed, living in thin tents. A soldier wrote home from Charleston, asking for a box of gingerbread, a little flour, butter and pods of red pepper for his Christmas dinner, which he would share with the "mess." He was fortunate to find some copies of the New Testament in a Charleston shop for Christmas presents for his children. At home, the children are made happy with rag dolls. Worn petticoats are torn into strips for bandages for the wounded; the ruffles of lace are ripped off and used for doll dresses. Old worn socks are unraveled and rolled into balls for the little boys, but this won't last. The war will soon be over. The South hopes on.

Christmas 1864: pots of black dye boiling all over the South, and there is mourning in every home after Cold Harbor, the bloodiest half-hour in history, but the South hopes on. A soldier in Charleston wrote, "Flour is $112 the barrel; meat $10 the pound," other foods in proportion. Fewer workers were now in the fields, and there was no money for farming supplies. The pigs butchered on the farm at Grandma's were divided with the army. Sausage and a mess of spare ribs with corn bread and turnips made up the Christmas feast. There were also dried peas, sweet potatoes, dried fruit and sorghum, but no flour, sugar, tea or coffee.

But Christmas is the inalienable right of childhood, even in time of war, and mothers contrived to give their children pleasure even though their own hearts were heavy with grief. If you had been a mother in 1864, you would have taxed your ingenuity in making Christmas happiness for your children. Grandma told of working far into the night to make cornhusk dolls for the little girls—there was not even a bit of cloth for doll dresses now. Gingerbread men were baked for the tots. Mothers made whistles for little boys out of willow branches. Older children were made to understand that they must be brave little soldiers and not expect gifts in war times. One little girl, just nine years old, hung up her stockings even though she had been told not to—and found it filled with switches.

"The memory of that ache in my heart occurs every Christmas morning, even now," the little girl of 1864 said at sixty-nine years of age.

When any of the soldier boys managed to get home for Christmas, there were balls and parties, as young people were starving for fun as a relief from sadness and sorrow. Girls cut up curtains and spreads to make into party gowns, and when all else failed, they wore calico gowns to parties. Eighty years later, American girls in war times were grumbling because they must wear rayon instead of nylon. How they needed to hear the story of Christmas in the Sixties as told by our own grandmother and passed down through the generations.

*Chapter 60*

# Hatpins

In the spring, a woman's fancy lightly turns to thoughts of hats. Right now, a tour of the hat shops is as thrilling as any garden tour; for color, for exquisite flowers, for sheer ecstasy, nothing equals the new spring hats. But in visiting my favorite hat shop recently, what should appear in view on a counter but a collection of hatpins?

Hatpins, did we say? Yes, the item that dated back to the past century when every lady's bedroom or boudoir where the dainty hats were kept, carefully shrouded in tissue paper, there also the indispensable hatpins. The hatpin of today is mostly for ornamental purposes, though why such lovely headgear should need additional ornaments is puzzling. But away back when, milady's hatpin was something absolutely essential whenever she donned her hat.

Hats were probably not made in exact head sizes then, as every hat in the late Nineties and early Naughts sat atop the puffs and rats, instead of fitting snugly around the head. Not many of the fashionable hats of this era need pinning on, and there is little chance of pinning on a hat to stay. The lady's crown of glory is clipped and curled with no long locks to keep the hat anchored by way of pins. Or else the modern girl's hair balloons out like an inflated balloon, and we would not know if a hatpin could find anything to hold to in the teased-up mass of hair. Anyway, the hatpins we saw recently were bits of jewelry, with glittering heads, all rhinestones, pearls, amethysts, pink glamor and all looking good enough to eat. Who would blame the girls for sticking one of the jeweled pins in their hats just to make for an atmosphere of romance?

Hatpins of other years were long enough to pin through the wide crowns of the huge hats. And since long, long locks had staying power for the pins, when the big hat had a yen to skitter off the pompadour on a windy day, it was held securely by the long pin. An ornamental hatpin holder on a lady's dressing table held her assortment of hatpins, mostly pins with white heads for white hats, black heads for dark hats and an occasional jeweled head for velvet hats with willow plumes.

The hatpin was a wicked-looking gadget, long and sharp. Of thin steel wire, it could serve two purposes in a pinch. When buggy riding in one of the stylish "hug-me-tights," if the Southern gentleman, who was not always so gentle as the romantic novels make like, was inclined to lean too close to the partner on the narrow buggy seat, the lady could remove her hatpin as quick as a wink, and no gentleman was brave enough to face such a weapon, which might be pointed toward his eye. As the late Judson Chapman once remarked pertaining to this aspect of hatpin protection, "There were wolves even in the good-old days."

There were two dark "kissing bridges" between Fairview/Beulah and Fairview/Pelzer in the 1880s. Young ladies may have needed hatpin protection. *Artist Art Frahm.*

The modern hatpins on display are not particularly designed for protection from the wolves with ulterior designs, and anyway, there is no time nor opportunity when speeding along a modern highway at a clip that would make any aim with a hatpin unsure. Then we wouldn't know if the modern miss needs a hatpin, what with highway patrols all along the way.

*Chapter 61*

# The Sack Dress

The original sack dress" was the sign above a unique item on display in a local antiques shop recently. We heard about the display and stopped by to see if the "original" would ring a bell in our memory. There was the display, as had been promised, and it did ring a bell. In fact, it did more than ring a bell: it painted a picture, but it was not an original dress.

Occupying a prominent place in a shop filled with treasures from the good old days was a garment made of unbleached homespun and trimmed with handmade embroidery edging at the neckline and armholes, a fashion in its heyday when Grandma was a girl and still favored in the Gay Nineties: the chemise. Not an original sack dress—the garment never had been a dress. The wearer of this handmade chemise would have been horrified had she seen what she designed for modesty's sake as "an extreme undergarment" hanging on the wall for the public to view.

Evidently, the garment in question was part of a bride's trousseau, as many hours had been spent in making that edging. A strip of the material from which the garment was cut was made into embroidery by means of punching tiny holes with a stiletto-like gadget. Then, with needle and thread, the hole was finely embroidered in a close stitch, leaving an open puncture in the center. Yards of such embroidery were painstakingly fashioned for adorning trousseau garments and even little girls' clothing. The embroidery on the chemise on display was yellowed with age, as was the material in the garment, but it is proof that the whole thing is authentic. We have seen many of these old-timers that were still being worn by older ladies in the

Nineties. The material of which they were made was practically wear-proof and wash-proof, lasting for years.

The sack dress, as originally worn, consisted of a sack or saque, worn as an overblouse with a skirt. The sack dress now in fashion looks more like a chemise and less like a sack. There were two patterns for the sack. Grandma and her older friends wore long black skirts and sacks. The sack was a kind of loose basque, and the skirt was gathered into a waistband, cut from yards and yards of cloth, a figure-concealing costume. They wore dress-up sacks of black silk or sateen and everyday sacks of figured percale or calico, with long sleeves and little collars fastened at the throat with a breast pin.

In the Naughts, the sack came in fashion as an informal overblouse for housewear or for maternity wear. This very modern sack was full and followed the same general lines of the "Butcher Boy" smock now in vogue for mothers-to-be. Grandma thought such loose-fitting sacks very immodest, though why we never could understand. The sack was then known as the dressing sack and was never worn outside the house save for maternity wear. We never saw in Grandma's day, nor in the Naughts after the revival of the sack, any loose-fitting dress called a "sack dress." The middy blouse–type dress now called a sack dress was in vogue in the Naughts and Teens, but the style now called the sack dress, a variation of the "extreme undergarment," was never seen in public in the more or less good old days.

## Chapter 62

# Confederate Mothers

Few things are more inspiring than life stories of the great mothers of all the ages. But for heroism under difficulties and patient endurance of hardship, the mothers in the South in the Sixties excelled against all the rest.

What would the modern mother do if she could buy no soda nor baking powder to put in biscuits, and if she had very little of the wherewithal for making bread, or if she could buy no salt, no sugar and no coffee?

What would a modern mother do if her children had to walk three miles to a little cabin school? What if her children had no shoes? What if she lived on a farm and her husband was away at the front and she had nobody to plow her fields?

Our Southern women faced these problems and many more, and somehow they learned to manage, to make do with what they had. Salt was one of the first commodities to vanish from the stores after a strict blockade was being enforced. How carefully every grain of salt was conserved! It was distasteful to dig up the dirt in the old smokehouse and try to sift out precious salt from the debris, but it had to be done.

Mothers burned corncobs to ashes, soaked the ashes in water and used the liquid thus derived as a substitute for soda.

Accustomed to beautifully appointed tables with elegant service by candlelight, mothers now gathered their children around the table to have their meals before dark. Candles were too scarce to be used save when absolutely necessary. A meal would consist of plain cornbread; vegetables, if any, from the home garden; bits of homegrown meat; and sweet potatoes. On nearly every farm, sweet potatoes were produced since they did not require much fertilizing and very little cultivation. Many a meal consisted solely of sweet potatoes roasted in the ashes of the fireplace. Eaten while fresh from the fireplace, the potatoes were delicious and nourishing.

Sorghum was used to sweeten the dried fruit for pies, and a potato pie sweetened with sorghum was a treat to the family. Always, there was the thought of saving food for dividing with the men in the army who had so little food. Southern mothers taught their children to think of the men at the front and to eat plain food thankfully, leaving any food thus saved to be sent to the starving soldiers.

Mothers wove coarse cotton fabric for clothing, but the serious problem was the lack of shoes. Grandma was advised in a letter from her husband to "have one of the cows butchered and save the hide. Mr. M. will make you a pair of shoes from the hide." The shoes made by the neighborhood cobbler from the cow's hide hastily tanned were not the elegant numbers that modern women wear. The outside of the shoes still gave evidence of the outside of the hide, but they kept the mother's feet warm when she was completing the arduous tasks that mothers were compelled to get done in war times. Mothers and daughters plaited husks of corn for hats, fashioned buttons from bits of gourds and wore home-woven frocks with handmade hats with the air of queens. Not even the shoes with some of the color of the brindle cow's hide showing embarrassed our Southern mothers. They were too busy developing substitutes for the heretofore simple articles needed in their homes, such as going to the woods for roots and barks to use in making medicines and

In the 1860s, mothers named children for Confederate heroes. Jefferson Davis McKittrick is seen with his first wife, Nancy "Nannie" Thackston. Circa 1895. *Authors' family collection.*

dyes. They were also going to the fields to keep the few faithful servants who remained from being discouraged with the hard work and unfamiliar conditions. Always there was hope that soon the war would be over, and all would be well again.

Southern mothers were of the stuff of which heroines are made It is fitting that they be honored on a day set apart for paying tribute to great mothers.

*Chapter 63*

# The Black Gum Toothbrush

Toothbrushes grew on trees, or at least the makings of toothbrushes could be found on trees and bushes in the woods surrounding the little country schools away back when. Possibly, there are boys and girls yet living who went to country schools in the Nineties and who recall the toothbrushes that grew on black gum bushes.

For some reason, the twigs of black gum were more resilient than other twigs and more fibrous, which made them ideal for the purpose of cleansing the teeth. We don't know who started it, but our grandmothers who went to school long before the war utilized black gum twigs for making toothbrushes, so doubtless the pioneer Americans originated the custom from necessity. Our ingenious early settlers soon became adept at improvising articles to fit their needs.

Somehow, the black gum grew in profusion around the schoolyards, and it was fun to break off a small branch from a gum bush and twist off a piece about five inches long. One end of the piece of twig was the handle of the toothbrush. At the other end, the fibers were treated by twisting and pulling until a tiny mat was formed. The fibers thus twisted into shape would not break nor grow stiff, so they made an ideal brush.

When using the toothbrush, one simply held the handle and applied the brush to the teeth and rubbed briskly over the teeth and gums. This little brush, grown on a bush or tree, not only kept teeth clean, but it also stimulated circulation in the gums and kept the mouth in good condition. The bark and fiber had a pleasant flavor, and nobody minded using the toothbrush.

During the dinner hour at school, children searched for the finest bushes of black gum and selected the right-sized twigs for material for dental aid. It was a normal sight, seeing boys and girls twisting the twigs and getting the fibrous mat in shape. Cleansing the teeth was not done in privacy; we went about the school grounds with black gum toothbrushes protruding from between the lips. We were not permitted to use them in the schoolroom, but outside, we were privileged to keep using the sweet-tasting brushes. Strange to say, no enterprising person ever went into the woods to cut down all the black gums and start a toothbrush factory. The gum trees grew unmolested for many a year, and generations of children continued to show good white teeth without any cost for dentifrices.

When "store" toothbrushes became the fashion, the old homemade numbers were discarded. Children were afraid of being laughed at if they held on to the outmoded black gum brushes. Still, a few diehards refused to spend good money for toothbrushes when the woods were full of them for free. The congregation of an old-time country church was asked to make their annual donation to an orphans' home in the form of toothbrushes for the children.

"I'm agin' it," sniffed one old-timer. "Let 'em use black gum toothbrushes like I did."

*Chapter 64*

# Brush-Arbor Church

The humming of bees overhead, the sounds of breezes in the pines and the long drawn out "Heee-ha-aw!" of a flop-eared mule weary of standing tethered to a tree were familiar sounds in the day of the brush-arbor church. A recent news story tells of a modern brush arbor having been erected by a group, earnest in their determination to worship according to their own faith, even though they had to go back to the customs of the pioneers to provide a place for worship services.

When our fathers came to the New World, they raised little log cabin homes for their families, and as soon as possible, they built log meetinghouses. Before they built the cabin churches, they worshipped in brush arbors when the weather would permit. Many of the little altar spots up and down the coast of the Atlantic are today great churches with large congregations, but originally these churches stemmed from the humble brush arbor in the wilderness.

All around the pioneers were riches of virgin pine and hardwood, building material to last for many generations. But before our fathers wielded the broad axe and shored up timbers for church buildings, they would select a site in the center of the little settlement and clear a little spot for the brush arbor. Great trees stood at the sides and the four corners. Men cut tops of thick pine, which was fairly good for keeping off the rain. These pine brushes were crisscrossed from bough to bough of the shade trees until a green roof overhead offered a degree of protection from the weather.

A huge section of a tree was placed for the pulpit, and logs were trimmed on one side and placed for benches. A chair was brought from one of the homes for the minister to use; and when brush and undergrowth was cleared from the premises, the place of worship was ready. Always, there was a nearby spring, just as every cabin home was erected near one of the many springs of clear, cold water. A wooden bucket with a tin dipper or a gourd for dipper stood near the log pulpit, and the preacher paused occasionally to refresh himself and ease the dryness in his throat with a long drink of spring water.

The plaintive notes of the old Songs of Zion floated out from the humble brush arbor and resounded in the forest. In early days, it was said that Indians sometime lurked in the forests and listened to the strange sounds of hymn singing. Sermons were long but earnest and powerful messages from the Gospel. Unsung heroes were those ministers in pioneer times who rode on horseback throughout the colonies, visiting the little brush arbors and log cabin churches, with a Bible in their saddlebags.

On horseback or on foot, the settlers would come for long distances when there was to be preaching at the brush arbor. Grandma heard it from her own grandmother that young girls would walk barefooted through the woods, carrying their shoes and stockings in order to save their shoes and have them looking nice when they reached the brush arbor. Before they arrived, they would sit down on a log and put on shoes and stockings. Properly shod, they would arrive looking their Sunday best.

It was a great day for a little congregation when their brush-arbor church was replaced by a new meetinghouse. Years later, the elderly people liked to tell of brush-arbor meetings when they were young.

# 1900s (Naughts)

# Chapter 65

# Protracted Meetings

Summertime was Protracted Meeting time in the early Naughts, and young people looked forward to this season as a time when they would go with their dates to meetings in all the community churches. There were several churches within buggy-riding distance, and each church had a time-honored, scheduled date for the Protracted Meeting.

Beginning the third Sunday in July, the meetings lasted in the several churches until late August. Young men kept track of the scheduled meetings, and each dated up his best girl weeks ahead. There were no air-conditioned churches then, and the girls dressed in cool, white organdy dresses, while the boys sweltered in blue serge suits with stiff collars. Sport shirts and other comfortable apparel for young men was unknown then.

But there were fans. Each girl carried her fan to church, and the white silk fan with ivory standards was as much a part of the dress-up costume as the earbobs are today. All over the church, there were young girls in lovely white dresses and young men in dark suits, the escorts each wielding his lady's fan. We wonder how it must have looked to the minister from his stand in the pulpit, a sea of white fans waving all over the church.

Naturally, the sweltering evening and the dark suits did not make for comfort, and the young men waved with all their might to keep up a semblance of cool atmosphere. The August lily, one of the sweetest flowers of the summer, was in bloom then, and nearly every girl wore an August lily bud, the fragrance wafted over the church by waving fans.

The couples drove in buggies along the country roads to church. Moonlight shining through the trees and the rhythmic beat of the horses' feet keeping time to slow-moving wheels made buggy driving to the Protracted Meeting one of the long-remembered pleasures of the good old summertime.

Yet these were serious occasions too. The revival sermons impressed the young people, and they all joined in the singing with strong, even if untrained, voices. Many a young person was saved during the Protracted Meeting, and all in all, the good old custom of the summer revival was well worthwhile.

One dear old minister who had no young people in his own family was soured on what he called the "social aspect" of the evening services. When the Protracted Meeting began in his church, he announced that there would be morning services only because he disliked seeing the meeting turned into a social occasion. Naturally, this minister lost all influence over young people in his church and other churches.

But time passed on, and the automobile replaced the horse and buggy. "Going to night meeting" was replaced by other interests, and a generation arose that found it hard to believe that their parents had ever thought driving in buggies to Protracted Meetings was something to look forward to in summertime.

In the 1980s, short-sleeves or sleeveless dresses replaced suits and collars. *From left to right*: Margie, Liz, Mary Caroline, Caroline, Agnes, Mary, Jean, Millie and Tom sweltered until Fairview Church installed air conditioning. *Authors' family collection.*

*Chapter 66*

# Lawn Parties

The old-fashioned lawn party of horse-and-buggy days was the last word in good times for the young people. Lawn parties and summertime were synonymous, and we could hardly wait for the season to arrive.

Every family had big lawns or shady yards, and along about July 1, every home where there were young girls had to be spruced up and ready for social occasions. The indoor parties with their strenuous games of Twistification and the like belonged to wintertime. The lawn party was for summer.

The young men in the rural neighborhood would eagerly plead with the girls to get up a lawn party, and when the girls' parents consented, all there was to do was to tell the boys to get word around to everybody in our social set. And "everybody" meant girls and boys from families for miles around.

The lawn was neatly clipped and the yard swept until it literally shone with cleanliness. Long benches were set up. These were simply stout planks with legs attached, long enough to hold at least two couples. Benches were placed under the boughs of the trees, and Japanese lanterns hanging from all the trees about the place made a very inviting scene.

In earlier days, no refreshments were expected. There was the water bucket with its dipper on the back porch, and it was fun to gather around and share the dipper. Later, it was the custom to have a big tub of lemonade free for all to help themselves. Also, there were sometimes fiddlers in the neighborhood to come and keep lively tunes going while the young people talked.

There was invariably a committee to keep changing the partners. After the girls had strolled around sweeping the ground with their filmy organdy or muslin frocks, each was invited to take a seat on one of the benches along with her partner. One of the committee soon approached with another young man at her elbow. The new young man was formally introduced, although the two might have made mud pies together and pulled each other's hair in former times.

The committee member then took charge of the girl's first partner, while the latest took his seat beside her. Around and around the lawn they went, introducing new partners, and every girl met every boy present and talked with him for an interval.

There were problems, such as some of the boys being "sticks" and an occasional girl being "dumb." In that case, a girl might get "stuck" with the undesirable partner, or the boy might want to leave the girl he was with. One pair of boys, good friends, had an arrangement whereby each watched the other for the "SOS" signal, which meant, "Get me out of this." The friend would kindly come to the rescue by yelling out, "Tom, your horse is loose!" Tom had to hurry to his horse, and the committee brought his dumb partner another boy.

The lawn party began soon after dark, and by 10:30, all were ready to start the buggy ride toward home. Flowers were by that time wilting in the girls' hair, and the long trailing frocks were showing signs of dew and dust. The moonlight drive along sandy roads and through covered bridges via the willow-bordered streams was out of this world.

The newest "older" generation (in their sixties) have lawn party fun in the 2000s. *Authors' family collection.*

## Chapter 67

# Pound Parties and Twistification

The approved custom of ushering in the New Year and saying farewell to the old was the staging of a pound party, which were still in vogue in rural sections in the Naughts. What with all the feasting during the week of Christmas, it would seem that everybody had grown weary of rich food. But young people liked sweets, and a pound party was the highlight of the winter season.

Word would go out all over the community: "There will be a pound party at the Blanks, and we will see the New Year in. Be sure and come." All the girls would know what was expected. Each girl who planned to go to the party would take a big cake, and each boy would bring candy or fruit.

The long dining room table in the home of the hostess would be laid with snowy damask, centered with an arrangement of holly and other greens and lighted with hanging lamps from overhead. As the guests trooped in, laden with big packages, the cakes were placed on the table and a sideboard or serving table would be made ready for candy and fruit. There would be a half dozen rich pound cakes, big coconut cakes, lemon cakes, marble cakes, Lady Baltimore and every kind of cake favored by families in that day. There would scarcely be an inch of the table not covered by cake dishes, while mounds of fruit and candy were piled on side tables.

Girls divested themselves of coats and fascinators and hurried to join the boys in living room and hall. The spacious hall would be ready for the games, with furniture removed and the floor polished.

The fiddler tuned up, and the young people hurried to line up for games. "Twistification" was a favorite, played to the music of the fiddles. Other games included singing games, and the words of the folk songs accompanied the fiddle music while the players went through the motions in perfect time. Strenuous games they were: such as "Old Dan Tucker," "Chase the Buffalo," "Turn Cinnamon Turn" and many others. Such folk games with songs should be rescued from near oblivion—they are real Americana.

By the time the players were puffing from near exhaustion, they would be called to come to supper. Filling the dining room, the young people would partake of the "pound supper" served picnic style. After they had eaten their fill of the various cakes and confections, the girls and boys were ready for more games. Youth is wonderful, and a supper of cake didn't stop their fun. Around and around they played and sang, until after eleven o'clock, an hour forbidden any other night. Ordinarily, the youngsters were required to break up their parties before eleven and start toward home.

As the final phase of the evening's fun, all would gather around the piano and join in singing any songs that came to mind. One person kept tab on the time, and as midnight approached, he would advise the crowd to quiet down and listen. Promptly with the first stroke of midnight, there would be loud cheering, shouts of "Happy New Year" and some youngster would start pulling the rope that swung from the plantation bell in the backyard. This bell was never rung except to call field hands from their work at noon, to summon the workers in early morning or in case of sudden illness in the family in the night, when the bell would be rung to notify neighbors to come to the aid of the family. As the old year died, it was permissible to ring in the New Year with the big bell, and it was great fun.

Soon, all were seeking coats, hats and fascinators and starting off on the moonlight drive over frosty roads—a fitting climax to the pound party for New Year's.

*Opposite, top*: Can you imagine these Sprouse cousins partying in their 1890s youth? *Authors' family collection.*

*Opposite, bottom*: Or can you envision their descendants dancing the Charleston in the 1920s or jitterbugging in the 1940–'50s? Will Sprouse and D.H. Garrett families. Circa 1964. *Authors' family collection.*

*Chapter 68*

# Beauty Aids in the Naughts

What to do about lipstick and is it safe or what not seems to be stirring up a mild tempest in circles that have a yen for finding something needing to be changed. But if we had any money to use one way or the other, we would use it on lipstick, users of which will probably keep on using the beauty aid whether or not the wise ones object.

Users of lipstick include practically every female, save those still in the cradle whose rosebud lips don't need enhancing. There are constantly changing fashions in lipstick, changing from deep red and dark purple to shades of pink and now white, in the same way there have been changing fashions in beauty aids since the day the first fig leaf apron was worn.

Girls in the Naughts had not heard of lipstick, but they were continually in search of aids to make themselves more attractive. It was the notion of older folks that "artificial" beauty aids were sinful. A girl should let her face and figure remain as nature designed them, in the opinion of Grandma and her generation. We had to slip when we wanted to make our cheeks more rosy than nature provided.

When our mothers were out of hearing of their own mothers, they reminded us that they used to go to the pasture for mullein leaves in their own girlhood. Mullein leaves were rough and fuzzy and when rubbed hard on the cheeks would produce glowing, rosy cheeks, the envy of the girls who hadn't applied mullein before going to a party.

Also, our mothers practiced biting their lips between sharp teeth to make their lips rosy to match their cheeks. If Grandma suspected some trick that she would call "sinful" to effect these ersatz roses, she never found out what it was.

Daughters of the mullein school of beauty practiced the art of soaking pieces of red fabric in cold water and daintily applying the red rags to cheeks to achieve a rosy effect—that is, the pale girls did that. Most of the girls in the Naughts were rosy enough for the prevailing fashion, which was for very fair skin. To achieve the fair skin was something that required many aids, artificial and natural. One had to wear big sunbonnets every time she stepped out of the house. Even small girls had to wear bonnets when playing outside for fear the sun would "ruin their complexions." A fair complexion was then considered a girl's chief claim to beauty, so little girls and older ones were martyrs to the fashion for untanned faces.

On their hands, when doing any gardening, they wore heavy gloves made by cutting off the toes of men's worn socks. "Keep your hands white," girls were continually admonished. Our mothers had sometimes been fortunate enough to slip into their rooms a bottle of "liquid complexion balm," which made faces look like they had been whitewashed. But in the Naughts, face powder, mostly known as "Swansdown," had become

Lipsticked mothers and lassies in 1999 trace ten matrilineal generations from Northern Ireland to the South Carolina Piedmont. *Authors' family collection.*

the fashion. Girls went around with faces powdered very white, which, without any color, rouge and lipstick must have looked unreal. By that time, mothers remembering their mullein days were relenting a little, and girls were not forbidden to apply "Swansdown."

When rouge first came in fashion, there was much ado about "painting faces." "Did you see that girl, she is nothing but a painted Jezebel," old-timers would exclaim in disgust.

"No nice girl would paint her face," was Grandma's opinion.

Yet somehow, the fashion was not outmoded, and girls kept on using rouge, just as later they kept on lipsticking their lips. Fingernail polish in bright red next came in fashion, and the same old controversy over "painted nails" raged fiercely. Nails kept on being colored until finally the fashion became less popular, and girls can paint or not paint their nails now, yet still not be considered hopelessly out of style.

# Glossary

Like Shakespeare's ancient poems, the language in *Five Petticoats* has changed over the centuries. These terms were common, grammatically and politically correct in the 1800s and 1900s South Carolina Piedmont. We want you to read the old-timey dialect but thought you would appreciate a few definitions. The **bold type** indicates **Scotch-Irish** and/or old **European** origins. Unfortunately, space did not allow us to define all the unfamiliar words.

## *Chapter 1*

DECALOGUE: derived from **French** and **Greek**; meant the Ten Commandments of the Christian Bible.

DOMESTIC: made in one's own house; in this instance, woven cloth.

FROCK: an upper coat or outer garment; in this case, a dress.

HUZZY/HUSSY: a bad or worthless woman of questionable morals.

LIMBS: the body was likened to a tree with arms and legs, as limbs. No true lady in Grandma's time showed her limbs.

MANNA: in Old Testament, miraculous food found by the Israelites wandering in the wilderness. In **Irish**, mann is wheat, bread or food.

MEETINGHOUSE: **Scotch-Irish** term for church or house of worship.

PEACH TREE SWITCH: a small flexible branch from the peach tree used to spank or "switch" children for discipline.

PETTICOAT: very full, half-slip worn under a dress; 1880s era required four to six yards of fabric, but present-day half-slips use as little as one-half to two yards.

SPECTACLES: eyeglasses to correct vision, usually made of wire frames and glass lenses.

SYLLABUB: an **English,** alcoholic, uncooked dessert drink of wine and milk, served by the Church of England/Episcopalians in the South Carolina Lowcountry, similar to today's eggnog. Piedmont/Upcountry Presbyterians did not serve alcohol in their (cooked, but not boiled) boiled custard, or syllabub, which was served in goblets as a dessert beverage.

## Chapter 2

FEATHER BED: mattress filled with feathers; very soft and fluffy.

HAMLET: a small village or little cluster of houses in the country.

## Chapter 3

COLORED (PEOPLE): racial classification of the 1700s, 1800s and 1900s for black Africans or their multiracial descendants; black is *negro* in **Spanish** and *niger* in **Latin.** The NAACP still uses "Colored" in its acronym. Grandma believed Colored, Negro, darkie, Auntie and Uncle were respectful terms. She forbid her family to say derogatory "n" words, and so did Muzzy until her death in 1969.

COMBINE: pronounced COM-bine; machine that cut and threshed grain; invented in 1836; a horse-drawn machine, later motorized.

NINETIES AND NAUGHTS: 1890s and 1900s; zero was pronounced "naught" (rhymes with ought). Some people said "aught" for zero.

STIRRING AROUND: **Scotch-Irish** colloquialism for busily moving around to get something done.

# Chapter 4

MUSLIN: a type of fine, woven cotton cloth, notable for its soft knotty surface. Today, a rough or loosely woven, inexpensive fabric.

POKE: a **Scotch-Irish** term for a small bag or sack.

TANSY: a bitter herb for digestion, headaches and flavoring food.

# Chapter 5

CANDLEMAS DAY: February 2; a church feast day using many lights, marked the midpoint of winter in **Scotland;** a hiring day on **Scotch-Irish** farms.

CHILBLAINS: sores on hands and feet produced by cold, rough weather.

FASCINATOR: originally a fine, lacy head covering such as a shawl, made from wool or lace. Today, a wiggly, feathered hair ornament.

NAINSOOK: a soft, finely-woven cotton cloth with a shiny surface on one side; used for lingerie and baby clothes; not manufactured anymore.

PLEURISY: inflammation of the pleura or membrane of the thorax, with fever, pain, difficult breathing and cough.

QUINSY: inflammation of the throat, particularly the tonsils.

TALLOW: animal fat from sheep, oxen and cattle.

# Chapter 7

CRASH: a plain, loose-weave fabric; made with rough yarn of linen, jute or hemp fibers.

DOBBIN: nickname for a quiet, plodding farm horse.

ISINGLASS: substance made of thin sheets of mica (a mineral) or from the dried air-bladders of fish; used for buggy/surrey windows.

OILCLOTH: tight-weave cotton fabric with a slick, shiny coating of boiled linseed oil to make it waterproof.

## Chapter 8

ARBUCKLE'S COFFEE: Pittsburgh brothers patented flavor-preserving, commercial coffee roasting in 1865; their pre-roasted beans were a major "convenience food" for Grandma.

JAVA OR RIO: generic for green coffee beans; 1880s coffee was grown in Indonesia's Java island and Rio, Brazil.

## Chapter 9

CLABBER: **Scotch-Irish** term for purposefully heat-soured milk; like kefir or yogurt today.

HOOPS: metal bands to hold the staves in churn and barrel making.

STAVE: thin, narrow pieces of wood to make churns and barrels.

## Chapter 10

COUNTERPANE: a **Scotch-Irish** term for a type of coverlet for a bed.

NOTTINGHAM LACE: flat, machine-made lace; manufactured in Nottingham, **England**.

Romany Patteran: a handmade, coded sign put along the road or on a fencepost.

tuck combs: combs with gripping teeth to hold a lady's hair or hat in place.

## Chapter 11

bung: a stopper for the hole of a cask or barrel; often a dried corncob.

castor oil: oil from the **West Indies** castor plant seeds; a laxative medicine.

## Chapter 12

switching around: when a person, usually female, walks around swinging her hips. (Grandma would not have approved.)

## Chapter 13

put on airs: behaving as if you are more important than you are; also called "highfalutin." (Grandma didn't approve of this, either.)

talking a blue streak: speaking quickly and at great length, barely pausing for breath.

## Chapter 14

cud: cows must chew food a second time to fully digest it; semi-processed food or cud is brought back up from their stomach and then leisurely chewed.

*Dr. Chase's Recipes*: an 1800s traveling physician who published a book of eight hundred recipes for human and animal health; the local doctor wasn't called unless these remedies failed.

GIMLET: a hand tool for drilling small holes.

# Chapter 15

ERSATZ: a substitute or imitation replacement.

LAWN: a lightweight, thin, plain-weave fabric of linen or cotton; frequently with a crisp finish.

PILLION: a cushion for a woman to sit on when riding behind someone on horseback.

SHIRTWAIST: a style of blouse; later, often attached to a skirt and called a shirt-waist dress.

TINTYPE: an early photographic process; the image appeared on a thin piece of tin.

# Chapter 17

MOTHERS IN ISRAEL: biblical term for early Hebrew matriarchs who led the community; **Scotch-Irish** designation for faithful Presbyterian women who taught others to love the Lord.

PILLARS OF THE CHURCH: active, highly regarded, supportive church leaders; i.e., those deacons, Sunday school teachers and financial contributors who hold the congregation upright and together.

## Chapter 19

DIVAN: a sofa.

## Chapter 24

CHITLINGS: intestines of a hog/pig; also spelled chitterlings, chitlins; you eat 'em or hate 'em.

CRACKLINGS: pork rinds or skins, fried hard, into crispy bits; used in cornbread. (Grandma and Muzzy loved crackling cornbread. So do new Southern chefs.)

MESS OF (OR MESSES OF): not a certain measurement, but a general food portion that would feed your family; derived from old **European** terms for cooked dishes, and/or people dining together; evolved into present military "mess halls." Don't confuse with, "She's a mess," meaning an interesting, funny character.

MIDDLING: bacon-like pieces between a pig/hog's shoulder and ham, which is the hip/butt. (This was the only time it was proper to say "butt.")

PONE: particular type/shape of cornbread; also a generic term for a piece of cornbread.

RENDERING: melting and clarifying hard fat into purified cooking lard, tallow or oil.

## Chapter 27

OAKEN PALINGS: **Scotch-Irish** term for stakes or slats of split oak wood; driven into the ground to make a picket fence around the house and yard.

## Chapter 28

FROWZY: unkempt and untidy appearance of people or things.

## Chapter 30

HAMBURG: now North Augusta, South Carolina area; on the Savannah River; a port and market for very important goods going to and from Georgia and South Carolina.

UPPITY: conceited; used since the 1700s.

## Chapter 31

MADSTONE: stone-like mass from a cud-chewing animal's stomach (cow, deer); treatment for "mad" dog or other rabid animal bites; boiled in milk and applied to wounds to draw out the poison; could be reused; handed down for generations.

ST. SWITHIN'S DAY: July 15; named for an Anglo-Saxon bishop; folklore predicted that the weather on July 15 would continue for forty days; a Southern version of Ground Hog Day.

## Chapter 32

ELBOW GREASE: a seventeenth-century **English** term originally meaning working hard at manual labor.

## Chapter 33

SPIDER: a cast-iron frying pan with three legs. Placed among/above lumpy coals in open-hearth cooking, it allows for safer, more stable, even-heated frying and baking.

# Chapter 34

BED TICKS: mattress cover; made of tightly woven cloth such as canvas.

# Chapter 38

IRON KING: brand of cast-iron stove; before stoves, cooks used open fireplace and/or brick ovens.

# Chapter 40

MAW: the jaw-like opening of the cotton gin; it separated the cottonseeds and cotton bolls from the soft cotton.

# Chapter 41

MUSTARD PLASTERS: a rag bandage spread with a semi-liquid mixture of powdered mustard seed; applied ("plastered") to the chest or abdomen; helped heal colds and coughs by increasing circulation; theoretically like capsaicin creams today.

# Chapter 43

CASTILE SOAP: originated in Castile, **Spain**; olive or laurel oil and brine process; milder than lye and animal-fat soap.

LYE: alkaline/base solution made from water and ashes; chemically: sodium hydroxide.

# Chapter 44

CHUCKING: to strike a very gentle blow, such as affectionate tapping under the chin or on the shoulder.

# Chapter 48

HANDS: helpers, manual workers, hired servants; literally: an extra pair of hands.

# Chapter 50

SLATE(S): a type of smooth, thin, flat rock, generally in four- by six-inch or seven- by ten-inch pieces, with wooden frames, used to write on with chalk at school, as paper was too expensive.

STICKIES: a South Carolina biscuit-dough dessert or snack somewhat like a cinnamon roll but cooked in an iron frying pan.

# Chapter 51

KNOCK UP: Muzzy's term for hurriedly preparing biscuits; derived from the previously lengthy process of kneading, knocking, whacking excess air out of "beaten biscuit"; the invention of double-acting baking powder in the late 1880s led to the fluffy, Southern/American biscuits we eat today.

MIEN: a certain look, mood and manner.

TEARING AROUND: moving as fast as you can; going here and there.

## Chapter 52

INFARE: **Scotch-Irish** wedding feast; the groom's parents provided this celebration party in their home on the day *after* the wedding instead of today's rehearsal dinner.

## Chapter 53

SENNA LEAVES: a medicinal herb to cure constipation; still in some laxatives today.

## Chapter 54

CONSUMPTION: lung disease; tuberculosis, TB for short.

FERRIS WAISTS: popular brand of corset; whalebone ribbing and fabric with buttons or hooks; from under the bust, down over the hips; social rules forbid ladies to go outside the home without wearing a corset; like Spanx and body shapers today.

## Chapter 55

COPPERAS: iron sulphate; used in dye and ink; treatment for anemia; a nutritional supplement.

POKEBERRY: a plant with dark, bluish-purple berries; used for dye; in early spring, edible leaves taste like spinach; poke salad or poke sallit; remember Elvis' song, "Poke Salad Annie."

## *Chapter 56*

COAT SUIT: fashion term for a style of tailored jacket with a skirt; usually made of the same fabric; today we would simply say a "suit."

LEGHORNS: hat style; made of fine **Italian** wheat straw, often with a wide brim; also a breed of chicken.

## *Chapter 58*

BLUE MASS: medicine made with mercury; widely prescribed for diverse ailments like toothaches, tuberculosis and worms.

CALOMEL: Mecurous chloride; a mercury preparation for yellow fever treatment.

NEURALGIA: stabbing, burning, severe pain that occurs along a damaged nerve; common in diabetes.

## *Chapter 60*

HUG-ME-TIGHT: a woman's short, usually sleeveless, close-fitting, knitted jacket; a sweater vest today.

WOLF: a lecherous male; not a gentleman around a lady; may have tried to kiss her or worse, without her permission.

## *Chapter 61*

BASQUE: a close fitting bodice; extended from shoulders to waist or hip.

BREASTPIN: ornamental brooch or pin worn at the throat or on the chest; may be used to close a dress, coat or blouse, instead of a button.

SATEEN: fabric made with a satin weave structure; produces a shiny but soft surface; now used for sheets.

## Chapter 63

BLACK GUM: native North American tree; also called sour gum or tupelo tree; genus Nyssa.

## Chapter 64

SONGS OF ZION: hymns based on the Bible's Psalms

## Chapter 65

PROTRACTED MEETINGS: a religious service continued for many successive days; a revival with long-winded preaching and songs.

# Scotch-Irish Terms and Phrases

Many readers/listeners will think these are "Southern" terms. They are more accurately classified as Scotch-Irish "ethnic," since they are derived from Scots and Scotch-Irish speech patterns. People in Fairview and surrounding communities of the South Carolina Piedmont used these phrases away back when, as well as today. You can hear these terms in other parts of the country among Scotch-Irish descendants, too, but without the "Southern drawl" accent. Some Southern euphemisms, colloquialisms and phrases are often thought to be poor English. They, too, may be proper Scottish or Scotch-Irish grammar from the 1700s and 1800s.

The following definitions are based on Scotch-Irish and English research, as well as our personal interpretations and regional experiences.

AW-RITE: Muzzy's greeting when answering the telephone; it meant "Hello, I'm here and listening."

BAD MAN: euphemism or evasive substitute for the devil; no one was permitted to say devil.

BAD PLACE: hell; no one was allowed to say hell or any "cuss" word. We knew Rhett Butler was *not* a Southern gentleman when he said "damn" in *Gone with the Wind*.

DINNA: Scottish and Irish term that meant did not or don't; used by Grandma McKittrick in 1880.

DONE IN: tired.

FIXING TO: getting ready to do something; also preparing something; as in fixing to go to town or fixing dinner, rather than making dinner, which is used in the Northern states.

GALLIVANT/GALLIVANTIN' AROUND: traveling, going somewhere else when you should be staying at home, as judged by Muzzy and her sister, Cinnie.

HIT A LICK: strike a blow.

ILL: bad tempered.

KIN: a blood relative.

LET ON: to mention; as in, "Don't let on that Mrs. So and So said…"

LIPPEN: Grandma used this term; it meant to trust. "It's best to lippen."

LICKING: a severe beating or really hard spanking. "I'm gonna give you a lickin'."

MAD AS A WET HEN: *really* mad. If you've ever seen a wet chicken, you'll understand how this term came about.

MANY'S THE TIME: often.

MIGHT CAN OR MIGHT COULD: possibly or probably; "I might can do this."

ON ACCOUNT OF: because; taking into consideration.

OVER YONDER: proper adverb to describe direction and/or distance. A "yon" hill is close; a "yonder" hill is farther away or in a different direction; still used in Scotland today.

PERSNICKETY: fussy and hard to please.

FAR PIECE: a long distance.

PINKIE: little finger.

POOR MOUTH: one who pleads poverty. "He's always poor mouthin'."

I RECKON: I suppose. "I reckon we can go."

SLIP OF A GIRL: young, growing girl.

SMIDGE, SMIDGEN: small amount. "Put a smidgen of butter on my biscuit."

SPEAK O' THE DEVIL: usually said when you are talking about someone and they appear but never said in Grandma's time.

SPARKING: dating.

SUNDAY-GO-TO-MEETING CLOTHES: best clothes, worn only for Sunday church services.

YA'LL, ALSO Y'ALL: short for you all or everyone.

YOUNG'UN: young one; a child.

# Scotch-Irish Southern Receipts (Recipes)

# 1700s CHRISTMAS CUSTARD WITH FROTHY TOPPING

*Ratio to Multiply or Reduce the Recipe:*
1 egg, 1+ cup rich milk, ¼–2 Tbl. sugar
*Makes 2 half-cup servings.*

## CUSTARD

2 quarts rich milk (whole milk and some cream)
8 egg yolks, beaten slightly
sugar to taste, about 1 cup or less

Begin heating milk, yolks and sugar on low, or easier, use a double-boiler.
Stir constantly until moderately thick, thicker than milk but not thick enough to eat with a spoon. Be patient. Don't turn up the heat. It will curdle. That's why a double-boiler helps.

## TOPPING

8 egg whites, beaten stiffly
fresh nutmeg

Dip egg whites, one spoonful at a time, into the hot custard. They will cook slightly and float back to the top. Refrigerate until very cold.
Pour Custard into wine glasses or goblets. Put a spoonful of Topping on each.
Grate fresh nutmeg on top. (Fresh is much tastier than nutmeg from a tin.)
*Makes 16 half-cup servings.*

## SOUTH CAROLINA SCOTCH-IRISH TRADITIONS

Descendants confirm that early Fairview settlers, including Rebecca Peden Stennis, have used this Scotch-Irish receipt since the 1700s. Their rural area didn't have refrigeration until the 1900s. They chilled the custard in the snow or springhouse. The receipt was handed down and is still used today. We like it less sweet and with a touch of Harvey's Bristol Cream Sherry, like the Sherry Chiffon Pie in Atlanta's *Frances Virginia Tea Room Cookbook*. The dietitian partner was a Fairview descendant, Mary Agnes Coleman New. (See the Resources section of this book for her cookbook.)

# 1880s SOUTH CAROLINA CHICKEN PIE

CHICKEN FILLING
4–5 lb. whole stewing hen or chicken,
  including giblets
1 Tbl. salt
water to cover
3 hard-cooked/boiled eggs, peeled

Put chicken, giblets, salt and water in a heavy iron or metal pot. Cover and simmer about two hours, until meat slips from bones, (or use a slow cooker).
Strain and save broth. Break bird into pieces. Pull off meat. Discard bones, skin and gristle.
Coarsely chop meat, giblets and eggs. This yields about 4 cups broth and 4–5 cups of Chicken Filling, minus some for the howling cat. Maybe more if you really pick the carcass clean.

CRUST
1 receipt, **RICH BISCUIT DOUGH** (see page 214) divided in two
1 stick butter
black pepper

Roll first dough piece fairly thin. Cut about half into long strips. Lay across bottom of 9x12 buttered casserole dish, about an inch apart. Roll the rest of that dough very thin. Cut into small pieces for the filling.
Roll second dough into a top crust. Save scraps for filling.

(continued on page 212)

## SOUTH CAROLINA SCOTCH-IRISH TRADITIONS

This was Fairview grandma Mary Ann Stennis McKittrick's company dish in the 1880s. You may think you don't like dark meat, "innards" or liver. However, these are what make old-timey, Southern chicken recipes so flavorful and distinctively Scotch-Irish. "Never waste a scrap of meat," her granddaughter wrote in a 1940s magazine. "Any chicken pie with carrots and peas is a sacrilegious, Yankee rendition! Get a whiff of this savory <u>Southern</u> dish a'baking, and you'll come running at the sound of the dinner bell."

Alternate layers in casserole: chicken filling, black pepper and dough pieces. End with chicken. Dot with butter.

Pour broth to cover. Add water if necessary.

Seal with top crust. Cut slits and prick with a fork. Pour any remaining broth into the slits so pie is <u>very</u> juicy, or else the pie will bake dry. (We put the casserole on a cookie sheet with sides, so it wouldn't drip in the oven.)

Bake at 450 degrees until top crust is golden brown. About 45–60 minutes. When baked, juice should be oozing out of the slits. If not, add more broth/water and slip back into the oven for a few minutes.

Serve very hot.

*Makes about 8–10 servings.*

# 1890s Big Iron Pot Dinner

1–2 lbs. pork spare ribs
water to barely cover
1 quart fresh string beans, strings
   removed and snapped into 1-inch
   pieces (or 1 frozen package, 16
   oz.)
6–10 Irish/white potatoes, peeled
   and cut into chunks if large-sized
8–12 small, whole fresh okra pods
   (or any fresh vegetable)
salt and black pepper

Cook ribs and vegetables in simmering water (or slow cooker) until tender. Skim off most of the fat. Put vegetables on platter. Garnish with ribs.

*Makes about 6 servings.*

Always served with:
Sliced cantaloupe and tomatoes in summer.
Sliced onions and pickled beets in winter.
Pot juices as "pot liquor" soup.
CRISPY LITTLE BISCUITS, or maybe cracklin' cornbread, to dunk in pot liquor.

## South Carolina Scotch-Irish Traditions

Like her 1890s neighbors, Grandma McKittrick used one large iron pot to "fix," not "make," the family meal. This "dinner" was their biggest meal, eaten in the middle of the day. They served informally, in a large crockery bowl or platter put right on the table. Their cooking was not particularly high in fat or unhealthy. Meat was merely a "garnish." One pound of meat fed a family of six. Today folks expect ¼ to ½ pound per person! Southern vegetables were the showpiece. There was always a garden. The vegetables in the pot were whatever was ready to pick: pole beans, string beans, turnips, tomatoes, okra, corn or potatoes. For some unknown reason, squash was always served alone.

# 1900s Rich Biscuit Dough for Crispy Little Biscuits (and South Carolina Chicken Pie)

4 cups plain flour, no need to sift (use only soft wheat flour like White Lily, Martha White or Swans Down Cake Flour)

2 tsp. salt

4 tsp. baking powder

8 Tbl. (½ cup) shortening (butter, lard or Crisco)

about ¾ cup rich milk (whole milk and cream)

Mix flour, salt and baking powder together.

Quickly cut shortening into flour with your hands, pastry cutter or a few short whirls of food processor. (Grandma would have approved of this time saver). Mixture should be pea-sized.

Add milk and quickly stir up into soft dough. Put on floured surface. Knead lightly.

Roll out very thin, a scant ½-inch thick. Cut into small biscuits; or crust and strips for pie.

Bake biscuits at 500 degrees until brown, about 8–10 minutes.
*Makes about 3½ dozen.* (We used Muzzy's old 2-inch cutter and froze some for later use)

## South Carolina Scotch-Irish Traditions:

Caroline "Muzzy" Sprouse Coleman "knocked up" these small, thin biscuits for every meal in the early 1900s. Although she was Scotch-Irish thrifty, she used *rich* milk, from her own cows. In the days before homogenization, this was the cream-laden part. It rose to the top of the crock. She scoffed at "blue john" or "bottom" milk (i.e. skim milk). "It doesn't make good biscuits!" She measured the milk with her little brown pitcher. It held about two cups. The pitcher survives in the authors' family collections. If you are not a good biscuit maker, try Marshall's Biscuits, made in Alabama, or Mary B's thin style made in Pensacola, Florida. Forget any other brand—these are close to Scotch-Irish homemade, and what a time saver!

# Resources

We used these resources. Tourists, historians, genealogists and researchers may find them useful also.

Authors' family collections, 1830 to present: includes Caroline Coleman's research papers, published and unpublished articles; Civil War letters, legal documents, correspondence, photographs, one-of-a-kind artifacts and cultural materials such as drawings, clothing, hats, gloves, crockery, farm tools, primitive and Victorian furniture, single-loom coverlets and linens.

Bickerton, Anthea. *American-English, English-American: A Two-way Glossary of Words in Daily Use on Both Sides of the Atlantic.* London: Abson Books, 1985.

*Chambers 2-in-1 Dictionary & Thesaurus.* Edinburgh: Chambers Harrap Publishers Ltd., 2008.

Coleman, Caroline S. *Five Petticoats on Sunday.* Greenville, SC: Hiott Press, 1962.

Coleman, Caroline S., and B.C. Givens. *History of Fountain Inn.* Fountain Inn, SC: Tribune-Times, Inc. 1965: Bookquest, reprinted November 2012.

Coleman, Millie Huff. *The South's Legendary Frances Virginia Tea Room Cook Book.* Atlanta, GA: Peachtree Publishers Limited, 1981: Mildred Huff Coleman, reprinted 1996.

*Faith, Food, Family and Friends Favorite Recipes*, *A Collection by Fairview Presbyterian Church*. Kearney, NE: Morris Press Cookbooks, 2006.

Garrett, Mary Lou Stewart, comp. *History of Fairview Presbyterian Church of Greenville County, South Carolina*. By order of the Session of Fairview Presbyterian Church. Fountain, SC: Apress, 1986.

Kean, Mary, comp. *Scottish-English, English-Scottish*. London: Abson Books, 1987.

Montgomery, Michael. *From Ulster to America: The Scotch-Irish Heritage of American English*. Belfast: Ulster Historical Foundation, www.ancestryireland.com, 2006.

*Noah Webster's First Edition of an American Dictionary of the English Language; 1828 edition*. Anaheim, CA: Foundation for American Christian Education, 1967.

Paden, James Mark, ed. *The Pedens of South Carolina: John Peden and Margaret McDill and Their Descendants in America, Volume One*. Salt Lake City, UT: Warren & Carmack Publishing, 2013.

*The Pedens of America: An Outline History of the Ancestry and Descendants of John Peden and Margaret McDill Peden*. Editions: 1768–1900 Eleanor M. Hewell; 1900–1960 John Peden, Lizzie Peden and Lila Peden Sprouse. Columbia, SC: State Printing Company, reprinted 1978.

Stoops, Martha Stennis Sprouse, with Mary Lou Stewart Garrett. "The Ancestors and Descendants of Warren Hill Sprouse and Martha Jane McKittrick Sprouse." Not copyrighted and unpublished.

## *Websites*

www.BookquestUsedBooks. Online and bookstore in Fountain Inn, SC. 29644. For out-of-print, as well as new, books on South Carolina history and authors.

www.fairviewpca.com. For Fairview Presbyterian Church photographs, visits, archives and museum. Reverend Peter Spink, pastor. Fountain Inn, South Carolina. Church Phone: 864-862-2403 Email: info@fairviewpca.com

www.familytreedna.com/public/peden. For the Peden/Paden Y-DNA Project.

www.fountaininnhistorycenter.org. For local archives and unusual history exhibits, including Mrs. Caroline S. Coleman's hat and typewriter, and her mentor Robert Quillen's typewriter and photographs.

www.southernfoodmillie.com, or cssherm@cox.net. To order *Scotch-Irish Life in the South Carolina Piedmont* or to arrange programs about Scotch-Irish-Southern food or history, such as "Dine, Dress, Drink and Drawl: How the South Became Southern" and "During the Civil War: Cornbread, Bacon and Barefoot," by M. Coleman and C. Sherman.

.

# About the Authors

**Caroline Smith Sherman**, eldest granddaughter and namesake of Caroline S. Coleman, is a former home economics teacher and retired certified Woman Owned Small Business owner (WOSB) with three Virginia offices. Her thirty years of sales and marketing led to a state board position in the National Association of Temporary Services. She testified as an independent/small business owner at the 1998 National Press conference, moderated by Senate majority leader Trent Lott (R-MS). In 1999, she testified at the National Labor Relations Board, Department of Labor, Washington, D.C.

Caroline spent her early childhood on Muzzy's farm with her mother and Uncles Broad and Bill, while her father, Smitty, was overseas. She played in the creeks and pastures with cousins, children and grandchildren of families who lived on Muzzy's place. She stole away up the path through cotton fields to talk to Mamie, who smoked a corncob pipe and made the best cornbread. Holidays and summers, the Georgia cousins arrived for Peden and Sprouse reunions.

Caroline graduated from Hillcrest High School and Limestone College in Gaffney, South Carolina, with a BS in home economics education. A charter member of the Fountain Inn History Center, she helped reprint *The History of Fountain Inn*.

She has one brother, Walter "Buzzy" Smith; two daughters, Mary Caroline Riner and Elizabeth Martin Patty; and three grandchildren: John, Elizabeth and George Siddall. Married to the now deceased Lewis E. Sherman, no kin to the Yankee general, she acquired five more children, ten grandchildren and five great-grandchildren.

Today, she lives in Virginia Beach. She is a member of Broad Bay Island Garden Club, Great Bridge Chapter of the Daughters of the American Revolution and the Museum of the Confederacy. Joining All Saints Episcopal Church to be with her husband, she is even more like her grandmother Muzzy. Both have been dunked and sprinkled, just not in that order.

**Mildred "Millie" Caroline Huff Coleman**, another namesake of grandmother Muzzy, was supposed to be called Caroline. But her cousin, best friend and co-author arrived first, leaving her with Mildred, her paternal grandmother's name.

A Southern Foodways "Her-storian," properly dressed in vintage hats and gloves, "Miss Millie" speaks at wildly diverse events: National Oral History and National Women's Studies conferences, Steamfest Steampunk Victorian Tea, the American Orient Express Train Tours and on WABE Public Radio.

Quoted in *USA Today*, *World Tea News* and *Southern Living Magazine*, she is author of *The South's Legendary Frances Virginia Tea Room Cookbook*.

She has an MA in women's studies and a BS in family and consumer sciences: food journalism and education, with radio/TV courses at Emerson College in Boston. She is a University of Georgia Family and Consumer Sciences "Distinguished Alumni."

She is certified in family and consumer sciences; is a member of Les Dames d'Escoffier International, International Association of Culinary Professionals and the Master 4-H Club; and a past president of the Georgia Nutrition Council.

She and her husband, Tom (forty-two years!), live in the Battle of Atlanta area, where her great-great-grandfather McKittrick died in 1864. They have a daughter, Carina; son, Nick; and granddaughter, Aria Belle Smith.

Caroline and Mildred are members of the Southern Foodways Alliance and enjoy "foodie" trips together. This doesn't help their diet, but they are having fun writing and speaking.

**Mary Caroline "Carrie" Sprouse Coleman** (1883–1969) was an extraordinary South Carolina writer, leader and popular speaker famous in her era. She attended Greenville Chicora College, graduating from Asheville Normal Teachers College in North Carolina in 1904.

Coleman's writing career began in 1912 with a column, "Little Town Talk," in her mentor, Robert Quillen's, paper, the *Fountain Inn Tribune*. He was a well-known American columnist/humorist. This resulted in countless awards for her public service and newspaper and magazine features throughout the United States. Coleman was a regular contributor to *SC State Magazine*'s Palmetto Profiles and *The Sandlapper*, where her article, "Robert Quillen: 'The Sage of Fountain Inn'" was chosen for *The Sandlapper*'s 1969 hardback edition.

She wrote an editorial page column, "Away Back When," for the *Greenville Piedmont*, culminating in her first book, *Five Petticoats on Sunday*. She coauthored the *History of Fountain Inn*. She continued to write until one month before her death at age eighty-six.

Married to Samuel Lewis Coleman, she was the mother of three daughters, twin sons, eleven grandchildren and one namesake great-grandchild at the time of her death.

Listed in *Who's Who of American Women*, Coleman received "The Star Scribe Award" in 1952 and 1954 from *The Progressive Farmer* (precursor to *Southern Living*); the Fountain Inn Rotary Club's Outstanding Citizenship Award; and was honorary South Carolina State president of the United Daughters of the Confederacy.

Coleman was a charter member and state officer of both the National League of American Pen Women and a member of the United Daughters of the Confederacy, as well as state and county historical societies and civic organizations.

Leaving the Presbyterian Church of her youth to join her husband's First Baptist congregation, she laughed, "I have been sprinkled, so I guess now I can be dunked."

www.ingramcontent.com/pod-product-compliance
Lightning Source LLC
Chambersburg PA
CBHW070359100426
42812CB00005B/1563